AMAZING GRACE

lopes and Memories *by* Thomas M. Columbus

University of Dayton
Dayton, Ohio

Design by Frank Pauer
Cover photograph by John Consoli
Back cover photograph by Larry Burgess

Amazing Grace is typeset in Avenir and ITC Berkeley Oldstyle Standard, a favorite of the author's.

ISBN-13   978-0-9828129-0-7
ISBN-10   0-982-81290-6

Printed by Greyden Press
2251 Arbor Boulevard
Dayton, OH 45439
www.greydenpress.com

Printed and bound in Dayton, Ohio

In his words, we see the face of God.

The theme of grace flows through the essays of Thomas M. Columbus, whose poignant and powerful columns have graced the *University of Dayton Quarterly* and *University of Dayton Magazine* for nearly two decades.

He writes what he calls "the stuff of everyday life and eternity, of sadness and of joy." He tells stories of hopes and memories, piety and basketball. And whether writing about the death of a university president or his 15-year-old son, he reminds us of God's amazing grace in our lives.

This collection culminates an extraordinary 43-year career at the University of Dayton. All proceeds from the sale of *Amazing Grace: Hopes and Memories* will benefit the Benjamin Taylor Columbus Scholarship Fund in memory of Tom's son who died in 1996 on a soccer field.

"God's grace is with us constantly, but most of us don't daily open our eyes to it," he writes. "Death, whatever else it may be, is an eye-opener. So are children. With our eyes open, we see beyond surfaces. In others, we see God."

Tom's essays have opened our eyes, allowing us to peer into how the University of Dayton experience has inspired our lives, into how we can find the sacred in the ordinary — from the "exhilaration of a mud-football game on Founders Field" to "the feeling of instant welcome on a Ghetto porch."

His work has garnered awards — more than two dozen national and countless regional honors. But that's not where he's made his mark.

He's made his mark in words that move us. In words that stand the test of time — and show us the grace of God.

—**Teri Rizvi**, associate vice president for university communications
and a colleague of Tom Columbus for 22 years

When I got the job as an editor in UD's publications office nearly a decade ago, I felt fortunate. It took me years to realize just how lucky I was to be working with Tom Columbus. In my first few years, I never understood why Tom didn't do much of what I called editing. He didn't change a lot of words or simplify my English major's style into the journalist's economic prose. Over time, I came to better know Tom, to know his careful mind, the example of his writing, his stories of Cleveland and its sorry sports teams, his appreciation of a good scotch with friends and insistence on getting out of the office at lunch, his occasional disappearances to serve the United Way, and his quiet example of compassion, curiosity, humor, love and devotion — to his craft, to knowledge, to mystery and to each of us. All I ever wanted was to write something good enough for his magazine. He was editing me all along, long before I ever put words on a page.

—**Matthew Dewald**, managing editor, *University of Dayton Magazine*

Tom, despite his devious sense of humor and the whole unfortunate misadventure with the crocodile and the basketball in the chapel, is as deft and creative an editor as there is in the vast field of university magazine editing. He made a periodical that you could not ignore, recycle easily, dismiss or put aside for reading when you were down with the flu. Issue after issue for years he handed the world the very best of Flyer flavor — spiritual zest, communal verve, intellectual and emotional and cultural and social epiphany, tears and joy, a sense of his beloved university as a place that mattered far beyond its ostensible boundaries. One of the great editors in his profession, which he would never admit; and I think we should just let the whole crocodile in the chapel thing go. He apologized profusely, and I don't see why you are bringing it up here again. Cut the man some slack. It was a mistake. We all make mistakes. Not at that level, admittedly, but still.

—**Brian Doyle**, editor, *Portland Magazine*, University of Portland

Whenever I receive a UD publication that Tom has edited or made a contribution to, I immediately go to see what he has written. It is always a rewarding read — touching profoundly human themes drawn out of the ordinariness of life at home, on the campus, or in the community and delivered with the subtle Columbus humor.

—**Brother Raymond L. Fitz, S.M.**, past president of University of Dayton

For the first 10 years of the *University of Dayton Quarterly*, Tom and I would drive to Richmond, Ind., for a press-check of the magazine as our printer began running an issue.

By that time there was little we could actually change about the issue. We'd have color adjusted here and there if needed, though Tom once noticed a page that was missing an entire column of copy. Good catch. So there was a lot of standing around or waiting downstairs for the revisions to catch up with our expectations.

On most days, we'd usually get to Richmond as dawn was breaking — or occasionally before — and breakfast was always part of the tour. Our usual stop was the Bob Evans on Route 40, but there were days when breakfast became lunch as printing problems put us even further behind.

And so we'd talk. In the car (when Tom wasn't nodding off), at the printer or over breakfast, we'd talk. But anymore, I have no idea what was said. I'm sure it was never all that extraordinary — it was conversation that any one of us might have had. It was just table talk.

Now I realize that everything Tom talked about is in these pages — all those hopes and memories, in column after column. It's a conversation among friends, and he could just as easily be sitting across from you.

You might even want to pick up the check.

—**Frank Pauer**, art director, *University of Dayton Quarterly*,
University of Dayton Magazine

It isn't easy steering a university magazine that examines the intellectual and the spiritual, that brings religion into the conversation, that juggles internal machinations with external appearances. And yet Tom has done that so gracefully. And these columns show why. Tom is honest in his communication. He's humble and true. He cares, he feels. He brings it home. He cuts through the extraneous and the added-on. He tells stories where he lives, and what he lives is a life and a faith that is real and personal to him. It makes him think, and it makes him want to share those thoughts with his readers, not to teach or preach, but to examine with him, to share his journey. And his readers are grateful to have come along for this enriching ride.

—**Kerry Temple**, editor, *Notre Dame Magazine*, Notre Dame University

SING GOD'S PRAISE

Amazing grace! How sweet the sound …

The congregation sang "Amazing Grace" as his earthly remains were carried into the church in a plain pine coffin. He had lived a simple life, using what he needed and sharing the rest with others.

But his death touched thousands. Vested priests of the Roman Catholic Church stood six rows deep to celebrate his Mass of Christian Burial. Politicians and corporate powers prayed shoulder to shoulder with secretaries and teachers.

To many a life of simplicity and great power would be inexplicable. To Father Raymond A. Roesch, S.M., such a life was what was expected of a Marianist priest chosen to lead the University of Dayton.

Perhaps it was his simplicity that enabled him, as he led this University through the troubled times of the '60s and '70s, to steer the calm course which Father James Heft described in Father Roesch's funeral homily. Whatever the source of his competence and strength, he was unquestionably the architect of the University of Dayton as a major university.

"At first I didn't feel a great sadness," one colleague remarked to me. "After all, one couldn't script a more complete life: He'd been a priest and a teacher, an administrator who built a university. And, when he retired, he got to be president of another one. And, when he retired again, he came home to Dayton.

"But it hit me when I saw one of the older brothers from Alumni Hall stop at the casket during the viewing in the chapel. He just stood there for the longest time with his hand on top of Father Roesch's."

A giant has passed.

Yet even the moment of our mourning reminds us of the timelessness of the belief that sustained him in his earthly life.

When we've been there ten thousand years,
Bright shining as the sun,
We've no less days to sing God's praise
Than when we'd first begun.

REMEMBER THE 'BUMS'?

I remember the "bums." That's what they were called when I was a young boy in the old Cleveland neighborhood, fondly known as Urban Renewal Area B.

People didn't talk to the bums much. But we brought sandwiches out to them by the alley fence. As children we had romantic ideas of these strange and foreign men, that they rode the rails off to exotic places. Then we moved to the suburbs and memories of "bums" faded along with streetcars and the soot of coal-fired steam locomotives.

Since then we've seen men on the moon, microchips in action, and the collapse of Soviet Communism.

We've also seen the proliferation of the homeless, many with shattered lives and lost ambition.

And we will see more.

The state of Ohio has revised its General Assistance Program so that if you're not old, not young, and not disabled, you'll get six months' aid and that's it. Nobody liked the old system; no one seems to have a better idea.

We in Montgomery County are better prepared than most communities. We have 430 beds for the homeless. But there are 6,000 people here on general assistance. And hospitals here, which absorb the costs of unpaid bills, can expect to absorb an additional $7 million a year. How much can hospitals and unpaid landlords and utility companies absorb? How much more can the churches and social agencies do?

Washington has passed the buck to Columbus which passed it onto the rest of us. Welfare was a lousy program. But in April, when the money begins to run out, do we go back to taking a "bum" a sandwich? It won't work in Cleveland. They've got 43,000 people on general assistance. There aren't enough alleys.

We need a better idea — or maybe lots of ideas, like those of Rose Wildenhaus and Dick McBride, who are fighting to save a neighborhood, or Nancy Bramlage, who coordinates the service of hundreds of UD students, or all those faculty and staff members and students and alumni who strive to make this world more liveable.

This issue brings you some of their stories. We'll bring you more.

A MAN OF IMMENSE POWER

At Tom Frericks' wake, some people waited in line for over two hours.

I went early to the chapel because I had promised to drive my 10-year-old to basketball practice and CCD class. And I remembered that, in talking to Tom once about youth sports, he had told me one regret he had about his career was the time it took away from his children.

He was a man of immense organizational power — whether he wielded it in University budget meetings or in shaping the future of the NCAA.

Yet, the one thread running through the thousands of stories being told of Tom in the days after his death is that of a person who always took the time for others, for his family and for all of us who knew him.

He took time for people, not their positions or their power. Like many others, I have memories of him taking time —

■ to listen to a former administrator who with faltering step and fading mind would wander the halls of St. Mary's and remember past achievements,

■ to comfort a groundskeeper who inarticulately mourned a vanished presence when that administrator died,

■ to talk to a former player — neither a standout on the court nor, in his career, what the world would call a success — whose phone call asking for tickets Tom interrupted a meeting to take personally. ...

He had attributes we call "old school." His drive to succeed was so intense it made him reconsider whether he should coach basketball. He had a sense of responsibility and of detail so thorough that the week he died he personally wrote to the NCAA resigning his chairmanship of the basketball committee. He was fiercely loyal to those who worked for him; he once asked our department if we needed any "muscle" in a disagreement we were having with another area.

These are attributes some of the young might call "paternalistic."

Everybody should have such a father.

EXALTING THE LOWLY

Attending Mass one recent Sunday I thought myself far away from the concerns of this issue of the *Quarterly* — minds enlivened by teaching and research, lives imperiled by alcohol or inspired by pilgrims, the birth of a child and the martyrdom of priests in El Salvador.

Then the priest at my suburban Dayton church introduced the guest homilist, Brother Peter Daino, S.M., as a "great friend of St. Albert Parish." The words jarred me a bit. The personable Brother Daino was obviously there not to be a friend but to beg the congregation to befriend the people whom he aids at the Marianists' IMANI project in Africa.

And indeed Brother Daino thanked the parishioners for the support of their tithing program. He reported that IMANI (which is both the Swahili word for "faith" and an acronym for Incentive from the Marianists to Assist the Needy to be Independent) is doing well. Its graduates get jobs. It now serves hundreds not scores.

Yet, Brother Daino said, his faith was recently tested. Five babies of mothers in the program recently died of AIDS or malnutrition, the causes of thousands of African deaths. One mother had named her child Peter Daino in recognition of a man who cared. Brother Daino, like Christians before him confronted with the enormity of evil in the world, asked "Why do I do what I do?" And off he went to pray. His prayers became filled with an image of Mary and her message of the lowly being exalted and the hungry being fed.

He returned to work. He keeps his faith.

So do those rebuilding the country of El Salvador. And those who came from around the world to pray with the Taizé brothers in Dayton. And those who work here at UD giving comfort to single mothers or counsel to students. And those who teach and seek knowledge.

In asking our help, they do not seek to be befriended. They offer themselves as friends. They do not solve the problem of evil. But they share with us their faith, so that the lowly shall be exalted and the hungry shall be fed.

'SO CLOSE TO STRANGERS'

"Sir! Sir! Can we have class outside this morning?"

The eager student yearning to be free was not an 18-year-old. Rather he was a professor at the University of Dayton who this spring spent days in a classroom in close quarters with other professors — many of very different backgrounds — talking of many things: "That book's too hard." "There aren't any positive women role models in that one." "Why's this so complicated?"

They presented material; they discussed it. Some might say they rambled and they bickered. "Vigorous discussion" was what Patrick Palermo, associate provost, termed it. Basically, they did what they want their students to do. They learned.

Each learned to see the world through the eyes of those with the backgrounds of different disciplines. Working, as one said, "so close to strangers," they learned to move beyond their strangeness to collaboration. They did what they want their students this fall to do. They learned together.

"They" are a vanguard, a group of English, history, philosophy and religious studies professors who this fall will, with a pilot group of a few hundred students, launch what may be the largest and most far-reaching academic endeavor in the history of the University of Dayton. They will implement the new "humanities base," the four-course foundation to UD's revised general education program, a program which in its emphasis on students achieving an integrated and coherent education and in its scope (required of everybody) may eclipse anything before attempted in U.S. higher education.

UD believes it can rival the education of liberal arts colleges at an institution already noted for rigorous professional training and research. The effort, in its scope and interdisciplinary collaboration, is revolutionary. But not all is new. As psychologist Linda Zalokar Lease, one of the women of '67 featured in this issue, said, her taking philosophy here was valuable in order "to understand why you do what you're doing, to understand what the needs of society are, what needs to be done in this world, and how do I fit my talents to it." Learning to make connections and to integrate knowledge is a UD tradition.

A PHONE CALL

Andria Chiodo, chair of the languages department, called me one day in early summer. A relatively new professor in the department, Francisco J. Peñas-Bermejo, excited by what he had read, had written an unsolicited review of a book by a longtime UD professor, Robert Conard. She thought we might be interested.

So, a few days later, through campus mail came a copy of the review and Conard's *Understanding Heinrich Böll* (University of South Carolina Press), a literary analysis of the Nobel Prize-winning German novelist. The review was as long as a *UDQ* feature article. I put them both on a far corner of my cluttered desk. Four months later, most of this issue of the *Quarterly* was written and put together. And there the book and review still sat.

I scanned through the review again, and out of discussions of themes and techniques jumped a passage: "For Böll, the present can only be understood from the past, a past that means Hitler, fascism, National Socialism, and war."

The present can only be understood from the past.

I then realized that you can read this issue of *UDQ* as an elaboration of that theme. You can read how a nation facing a future with hope can learn from the horrors of the past. Or how a woman striving to learn to read and write is driven by images of her past and hope for her children. Or how UD alumni use half-forgotten melodies to help heal individuals with shattered pasts. Or how the members of a pilgrim church are faring, a generation after Vatican II.

And, in the *President's Report*, you can read how faculty and students are making connections across time (as well as space and culture).

The excitement of such connections may be why Böll won a Nobel Prize, why Conard wrote about Böll, why Peñas-Bermejo reviewed the work, and — I surmise — why Chiodo called me.

PIETY AND BASKETBALL

Thousands prayed at Holy Name rallies. Throngs filled the Fieldhouse to cheer Blackburn's Flyers. The 1950s were a time for basketball and piety.

As UD grew and prospered, we wanted to be seen as more than athletes and churchgoers. We were a real University with outstanding students, significant scholars and world-class researchers. And we are.

Nevertheless, on Dec. 8, 1992, the Feast of the Immaculate Conception of Mary, basketball and piety were back on center stage. In the afternoon, at the UD Arena, University officials announced UD's intention to join the Great Midwest Conference and return to basketball prominence. In the evening, at the Frericks Center (the former Fieldhouse) where thousands had cheered athletic heroes, thousands now were singing God's praises during the annual Christmas on Campus Mass.

Basketball and piety have never left UD. Even in this season when fans are filled more with sympathy and hope than with enthusiasm, Flyer basketball still draws greater numbers than any other UD — or Dayton-area — event. And on the core campus, nothing — not even the biggest Ghetto party — attracts more students than the Christmas on Campus Mass. Although the nation's outstanding Protestant universities as they moved to greatness largely abandoned their religious roots, UD has not.

But the Dec. 8th sermon, preached by the basketball chaplain, was neither complacent nor comforting. The words confronted the congregation, convivial in the joy of the day, with a world where people in India and Yugoslavia were killing each other in the name of religion, with a church that espouses justice but is seen denying it to women, and with a campus where a student can be hassled for the color of his skin.

But the Word need not have been made flesh if this world were perfect. Gathering together to play and to pray will not make it perfect, but in those gatherings is the community that is UD's tradition — and its hope.

AT THE BOARD MEETING

Soon after we learned that senior editors of higher education's primary trade publication had named *UDQ* the best of its kind (external audience tabloid), Brother Fitz asked Teri Rizvi, director of public relations, and me to appear at a meeting of the board of trustees.

For us, it was an honor. For the trustees, it was an accounting of stewardship from the staff. The trustees in 1990 had approved Brother Fitz's "Agenda for Excellence," a long-range vision for the University. To move toward that vision, they also committed substantial resources to the advancement division (alumni and parent relations, development, and public relations) in a plan called "Investment in Advancement."

The award is a return on that investment.

The award bears significance because, like the success of our alumni and parent programs and of our fund-raising efforts, it indicates professional competence. But, as we were able to tell the trustees, it signifies more. It signifies the success of the University.

Platitudes, no matter how well presented, do not impress the editors of *The Chronicle of Higher Education*. Substance does. They know reality is complex. And we have been fortunate to deal with it as such, to tell the stories of those who devote their lives to the mission of the University.

On Page 6, we briefly honor five recently deceased members of the UD community. The names — Baker, Donatelli, Huth, Leahy and Wisch — in death evoke many memories, but all with the common thread of individuals who confronted the complexity of a modern, Catholic university and strove to leave UD the better for their having been here.

They struggled with the complexity of reality, its paradoxes and perplexities. In this issue, you will read how their successors continue the struggle, dealing with issues ranging from national defense to the national pastime. In such efforts is the substance of the University.

It's a substantial return on investment.

COMPASSION AND RESPECT

"Jesus wept."

That sentence of John the Evangelist is, for me, perhaps the most evocative ever written. Confronted with the death of his friend Lazarus, Jesus — the Son of God all-powerful — weeps.

John's words intensely reveal the humanity of Jesus, the mystery of the Incarnation. Any of us who has yielded to death a person whom we loved knows what Jesus felt. And St. John's forceful sentence tells us that Jesus knows what we feel.

This publication conveys to our readers news of the deaths of persons related to the UD community. We list the names of many individuals under the heading "In Memoriam." For some widely known persons active at the University, we craft a few simple sentences.

When several members of the University died before our last issue, a colleague asked me if I were going to write a column that would make her cry. I couldn't. I had written, within one year, of Roesch and Frericks. And how could I do any justice to each of those who recently died without some slight to another? A few words cannot provide a fitting tribute to a human life. We can, for the most part, only inform and let each in his or her heart provide what human memorial is possible.

Yet a simple listing seems cold — as an alumnus writes, without "compassion and respect." But to do more than identify can mislead. We could add rank and title or list more relatives. But that would not capture what is lost — the person we sat next to in class or drank beer with, or a roommate's mother who filled a lonely weekend with homemade spaghetti, or the friend we'd meant for years to call. Our few lines — like the sympathy card or the hug at the funeral home — are destined to be inadequate gestures.

Yet, though we cannot share the intensity of each other's pain, we do share the loss. What Jesus felt at the tomb of his friend Lazarus is the stuff of our humanity.

EXPERIENCE BEYOND WORDS

In preparing to draft an honorary degree citation for Elie Wiesel, I was reading his book *Night*. I opened my dictionary to look up an unfamiliar word. It wasn't there. But one entry lept off the page: "leveraged buyout."

I was disconcerted at the mental juxtaposition. The Wiesel passage I was reading described an event in a concentration camp — the slow death by hanging of a young boy who had dared to hope for a better future. Wiesel heard a man there ask: "Where is God now?" and a voice within him answer, "Hanging here on this gallows."

The week that followed brought me many questions: Has the spiritual life of our nation been drowned in a material sea? Since words fall short of experience, can we comprehend at all the experience of such evil as the Holocaust? Can faith so shattered return to hope?

Those of us maturing in the late '50s and early '60s naively saw ourselves as a generation of hope, of Camelot and King, of desegregation and civil rights, of Vatican II and a pope who threw open a window.

The hope for America now sometimes seems less euphoric as we read today's news: skinheads here are not as violent as their skull-crushing European counterparts; book-burnings aren't widespread; and Klan rallies are not as well attended as rock concerts.

When Elie Wiesel was 12, a learned man of his town who had been taken away by soldiers returned to warn of death and burning bodies. The town ignored his warning.

Wiesel spoke at UD on a sunny Sunday. Later that day, as I watched my 12-year-old son take to the soccer field, I felt fear for his future, fear that the warning and the witness of Elie Wiesel may have been in vain. And I looked for hope. On campus, I see beginnings: in a faculty whose Dayton Plan poses the question of what it means to be human, in students struggling to grasp Wiesel's message, in one human being trying to understand another.

For there must be hope. The future has no alternative.

A RARE AND FRAGILE LIFE

One stormy January evening, our phone rang. Our son Mike, a UD senior, was calling to let us know the car in which he and his friends were riding on their way back to campus after a long weekend had broken down on I-70.

A week later at dinner with family friends, someone mentioned unconfirmed rumors that UD students returning to campus the previous week ran off the road to avoid an accident and totaled their car. Mike confirmed the rumor. "When I said we broke down, I was understating." His friend's sturdy Ford Explorer flipped; its square frame became rhomboid — but no one was hurt.

The incident recalled less comforting phone calls in the night. But this reminder of life's fragility also stressed the rare beauty of its relationships.

So, it's not unusual that alumni of the last decade or so whom we asked what they remember most about UD pointed invariably to relationships — with friends to whom they were close for years or friends with whom they just shared the exhilaration of a mud-football game on Founders Field or the feeling of instant welcome on a Ghetto porch.

Other stories in this issue also treat UD people and their relationships: Father Burns, who has affected thousands of husbands and wives; Brother Fitz, who sets a tone for the University by the way he lives and the way he listens; the thousands whose lives have intersected in Kennedy Union. …

One value of a UD education lies in having learned to appreciate such relationships. Evidence of this appreciation struck me a couple weeks ago. Immersed in such '90s work as writing stories of cost containment and developing publications to increase revenue, I opened a note from a graduate. She enclosed a clipping about the sudden death in a traffic accident of a fellow alumnus she described as "a true humanitarian and a good, decent man who loved his family. Although I didn't know him personally, I felt a true kinship with him because of UD."

I think a place and a people like that are a kinship worth claiming.

A COMPROMISING POSITION

We'll get letters.

Readers write them when we touch a nerve. To reach your nerves, this issue features religion, race relations and international trade. If that's not enough, we also have basketball, lawyers and college food.

The stories raise questions of compromise and accommodation, of identity and independence. How can a nation surrender some of its power to secure a better economic future? How can a university maintain a top-flight athletic program? How can a handful of black students on a predominantly white campus nurture their African-American cultural heritage?

When is compromise fruitful? Can a nation or an individual compromise and still maintain an identity?

Reading of UD's African-American students struggling with preserving their identity and culture made me think of my ancestors, of their cultures, of the languages they spoke and I do not. The so-called melting pot, however good-intentioned, destroyed strands of my cultural heritage. Of course, I realize that if the English royal family — yielding to the anti-German hysteria of 1917 — changed its Germanic name to Windsor, German immigrants in America would hardly pass to their children their native tongue.

When to yield, when to hold on, how to judge — these are complicated, often unclear, questions. Take the seemingly simple choice of the decorative words on our centerspread. The English translation of the final psalm is euphonious — but gender-specific in pronouns for God. This occasioned much office discussion. Within an article, we would have paraphrased or sought a different translation. But the traditional translation seems to better fit the 19th-century chapel art prominent in the spread's photographs.

If you disagree, tell us about it. Also, tell us your other thoughts on religion, race and trade — and basketball, lawyers and food. Strong beliefs don't hurt. After all, if my ancestors had clung more closely to their cultures, I'd be able to speak German and French and Welsh — and struggle with pronouns in all.

An Inconvenient Colleague

Until July 22, Kate Cassidy '87 occupied the office next to mine, there editing *Campus Report* and writing features for *UDQ* as well as producing its sports section. We had, as the cliché goes, an enjoyable working relationship — or, as a colleague put it, "they bickered all day."

I prefer to see it as a creative synergy that helped mold *UDQ* into the nation's best college tabloid. Other UD graduates should be proud and thankful for how forcefully and bluntly Kate represented their interests in our editiorial sessions. When visionary rhetoric would threaten to soar untethered, Kate — with a well-chosen word or two ("puke" comes to mind) — would bring us back to the complex reality that is a university experience.

Rationally, I accept her decision to move on — new horizons, growth and development and all that. But, as an editor and friend, I find it decidedly inconvenient. So, I cannot easily forgive Kate for leaving. I am of an age that I cling to past relationships, to comfort and stability — and to good writing.

We've talked about visiting; she's invited her office colleagues out to the desert. We may go.

We speculated on one grand plan of travel — get a bus, fill it with the whole PR staff and drive across the country doing stories, Charles Kuralt-style, on hundreds of UD alumni along the way.

But reality suggests the visit may be put off. Like the dinner that a friend and I planned at our 20th college class reunion. At our 25th we remembered our unfulfilled plan. Or like the intended visits to a couple who moved to Columbus. They had a baby when I last saw them — she's now in school, and another unseen by me has been born.

So our mass trip to Arizona, to a rational person, seems doubtful.

But who knows? We are driven by forces beyond reason. So maybe someday we'll be on that bus. Maybe we will drive off — to recapture our past and to seize our future. Maybe we can do both.

Maybe.

DECADES OF OUR LIVES

Suzanne's eyes were moist when I came home.

My day at the office had been particularly frustrating — balancing the 32 pages of this *UDQ* with 16 pages of a presidentially inspired vision of 2005. I was to the edge of questioning why, although Brother Fitz is a very nice man, worry about a decade away when next week is a mess?

And now at home, what? Happily, it was no disaster, as I recognized from the VCR remote in Suzanne's hand — my wife was watching the recently received videotape of the wedding of Elizabeth, our daughter. Focusing decades of our lives into a few hours, weddings, not surprisingly, confront us emotionally with growth and change, development and mortality, life and love. I had survived the event — just as I had Liz's moves from home to the world of Marycrest, Chambers and Alberta — with male stoicism and moved on, I thought.

A few weeks later, Liz called. Plans made months ago for her husband's large family reunion in another state conflicted with a tournament championship soccer game for the junior high school team she coaches. She had to leave at halftime to reach the reunion dinner on time. All the other coaches at school were busy. She and I had for years coached her younger brother's teams. How about coming out of retirement, Dad?

So, I did. I stood and watched her coach the first half. When her husband arrived sometime into the second half, she said, "I guess it's time to leave."

He replied, "I'm late. I was doing the laundry. [Smart lad.] Let's stay until the end of the game. [Very smart lad.]"

So we watched. For now there was nothing for me to do. The child I had held in my arms — it seems like just a few days ago — was on her own and masterful. The ending was scripted like an old movie — after two overtimes her team won in penalty kicks. And she and her husband drove off.

And I thought of the decades we mortals take to share and to plan, to shape our futures and to adapt to them. And, in the stillness of that autumn afternoon, I thought of how fast those decades go by.

Outward Signs

People here have been dreaming of their jobs lately. The other night I dreamed of a story shoved by hectic daily work to a very back burner, a photo spread on sacraments, the outward embodiments of the inner mystery of grace.

In my dream, looking for a way to do the story, I opened the chapel door. I saw a full congregation, facing west and raptly attentive to a prayer service and dramatic reading led by Jim Heft and Tony Macklin. Even in a dream, the juxtaposition of Marianist priest and iconoclastic professor seemed odd to me, but not to the congregation, perhaps a wise community who understood this meeting of administrator and maverick.

Also, as we rushed to print, I was involved in a waking experience of community — the confirmation of my younger son in the Roman Catholic Church. To some, that event may appear no stranger than my dream. For example, Benjamin chose, as his confirmation name, Robert, some homage to my father, but mostly to soccer great Roberto Baggio — an Italian convert to Buddhism.

From Ben's parents' viewpoint, the process leading to confirmation was often a series of prosaic questions: McDonald's or leftovers to make religious education classes on time? Can he miss a class for the big game? How can they expect us to remember where we put that baptismal candle?

But through the commonplace comes reflection — on the baby who now literally looks down on us, on the words "ventricular septal defect" that drove fear into our hearts, on joy at the unearned luck of the hole in the child's heart being too small to limit his physical activity, on the mysterious relationship of two parents and a young man as he joins the adult Christian community.

This dream, this experience — both point to a vision and a hope, mysterious and ever present. Unlike the great Gatsby's vision, a green light of hope unreachable by us "boats against the current, borne back ceaselessly into the past," the Christian vision transcends time. Our future is not only in our past but in our every present moment, drawing us ceaselessly to one another through the transforming gift of grace.

A TIME FOR POLKAS

I was heading home, having received the news that *UDQ* was sharing with Duke's magazine (and had beaten Yale's for) a prestigious award for reporting on issues in higher education.

Not bad for some writers who, partly because of the common thread of a Catholic childhood, had come together at a Midwestern Catholic university. Not bad for that University, whose openness in discussing issues fatally wounds the claim that "Catholic university" is an oxymoron.

Getting into the car that day, I reached for a cassette tape. I had seren-dipitously borrowed from the public library several that echoed my heritag-es, whether of heredity, geography or just spiritual affinity. I could choose from Irish or German, Cajun or country or blues. I picked the Polka King of the 1950s, Frankie Yankovic.

Most stereotypical allusions to the 1950s recall nothing to me. But mu-sic is different. A few minutes of that now-out-of-flavor music brought an explosion of images to mind: mid-century Cleveland — the wealth of steel and oil and the sweat of immigrants and migrants who built the wealth, who gathered round oil-cloth-covered kitchen tables, who together and in solitary fear prayed with faith that their children would have a future free of War and Depression.

Such fears are now largely the province of the aged, whose anniversaries we celebrate and set aside. For our time is now; we have our own achieve-ments. Certainly as an institution, UD has gained a secure level of academic prestige.

One UD professor fondly tells a childhood story of a good sister teach-ing his class in grade school to pronounce "coupon" correctly — so the young Catholics could play without social stigma among the other children. UD has grown to a University that can play with anybody, even the big kids.

But as we do, let's remember the fears, the hopes, the faith of those who went before. Then, more than just burying the phrase "Catholic university" as an oxymoron, we will have raised it to become a model of the harmony in truth of faith and reason.

TIMELESS IMAGES OF YOUTH

Memories of our youth return years later, more vivid than in the original perception. Perhaps that's a reason for the existence of alumni periodicals.

Recently I've remembered a brief glimpse I once caught of my father — unawares, alone, kneeling at his bed, hands clasped in prayer.

Today, I still can't categorize my feelings then: prayer is good, but my youth saw little value in solitary prayer, let alone in kneeling. Why he prayed so is among the questions I never asked him before he died. Perhaps as a child I could not formulate the words. Perhaps as an adult I was too proud of my skill with words to form an artless, awkward question. Most likely, life just became too busy and the question's importance faded.

Coincidence has since given me the task of often reflecting on those who have died. The first two issues of this periodical marked the deaths of Raymond Roesch and Tom Frericks — one the president when I began work at UD, the other the vice president who gave me my first communications job here. In this issue, I reflect on the life of Len Mann, dean of the College when I started teaching.

I face reality through words. Through their symbols and metaphors, their allusions and cadences, they can bring us some understanding, perhaps some peace. They can help us from the profane to the holy. Yet, they have limits; they are simply signs, tools of a greater reality. Any loving parent can find as much holiness in changing his child's diaper as in the statements of humanity's greatest works.

Perhaps that's why another image often returns to me. After my wife's mother died and was buried, I went to her old apartment to make sure it was cleaned out. There was nothing visible there — and yet there was still the indescribable feeling of a bond to a loving human being, even if absent from us now. I understood then something of my father.

And so, in a bare room in an empty apartment, alone, I knelt and tearfully and wordlessly prayed.

YOUTH, BASEBALL AND VISION

My colleagues call me predictable.

Admittedly, I am in my third decade of working for the same institution, living in the same city and being married to the same person. Every morning, I drink coffee before trying to mumble anything intelligible. I don't promise anybody anything.

Because I don't, when everybody said I would write about Cleveland, I didn't say I would. All I knew was — given the *President's Report* on Vision 2005 — I would write something on the future. They knew it would be Cleveland.

Even though I sometimes (well, all day) act the skeptic, questioning facts, ridiculing buzzwords and deflating silly optimism, they know that, beneath that exterior of an aging curmudgeon, burns the faith of an incurable idealist with an unquenchable hope in the future.

That's the fault of the Cleveland Indians.

It happened in the 1950s. As a child I learned to believe in skill and teamwork by watching them. I learned to read by following them in the local papers and *The Sporting News*. I learned math by tracking their averages and standings — where I learned disappointment by seeing too often my graphs depict the Indians' line sink below that of the Yankees. But that's how I also learned hope.

When a 1995 World Series ticket presented itself, I knew I must go. As I drove in on I-71, the belching Ford plant and the rejuvenated Flats spurred memories. Others may find their Arcadias in sweet meadows; the strongest image of my youth is dirty smoke pouring out of a steam engine churning its way under the Fulton Road bridge.

OK, so we lost the game and the Series. But we'll be back. Because in Cleveland the game is still fun and the fans have hope.

At Jacobs Field I met a Yankees fan who, looking around, said, "This is what the Yankees need."

Everybody does.

BEYOND DEATH'S CLICHÉS

When I was a young man, I thought the behavior of older people at funeral homes was odd. They'd greet friends they hadn't seen lately. They'd talk of old times. They'd go home and make casseroles. You'd think they were going to a baptism or a wedding.

As I grew older, I understood their talk a little better. The old know death is common. They know it is our fate. They know words of comfort and condolence, though they must be spoken, do not heal the loss.

With a community of 80,000 readers, *UDQ* has a similar weakness. We write in commemoration of the life of a Roesch or Frericks, known to all, but the rest of us have a simple In Memoriam. I apologize frequently to readers who wish for more for those they have loved. And all who die deserve something more, but obituaries are shallow reflections of life.

Last year a local youth, an outstanding athlete and student, was caught in a sudden thunderstorm and, as he tried to make his way home, was struck by lightning and died. My eighth-grader came home and told me of the wordless reaction of those at his school as they learned the news. He described one of the dead boy's friends, himself a star athlete, sitting in the hallway and crying. And I thought to myself: What else could he do?

This year, as tears turned to memories, the local high school held a benefit for a memorial scholarship. Not many days later, Chris Daniels died — and this far-flung Flyer community wept and raged and questioned and spoke the clichés of shock and sorrow, which though true, cannot console. What do you say to a mother who's lost her son, a teammate who's lost a friend?

So we gathered and we prayed. We've come together to remember, and in remembering maybe we're now the better. At a campus memorial Mass for Daniels, Father Gene Contadino, S.M., told the congregation, mostly young and tearful, "We come to say yes to God, to life and to each other."

For not in words, but in committing passionately to life and to each other, and thus to God, can we find any meaning in the face of death.

FAREWELL TO FAMILY?

Erma Bombeck is dead.

Father Burns has retired.

A wise professor once told me you sometimes don't know you've lost something until well after it is gone. He hoped the open, welcoming, loving spirit of the UD family wouldn't become such a loss. But "the old order changeth, yielding way to new," said Tennyson's King Arthur as his death approached.

Bombeck's death at 69 and Burns' retirement at 72 could raise fear that our personal loss will be aggravated by the institution somehow becoming the less.

Erma Bombeck '49 was the nation's favorite humorist. She was also the archetypal UD student: down-to-earth, considering herself lucky to be in college, looking for a place to be welcomed and finding it. Then she spent a career seeing life as it really is and sharing that with us. I hope God found a high place in heaven for Brother Tom Price who gave the young Erma those sustaining words, "You can write."

Norbert Burns '45 also knows the power of getting people to realize their own worth. He has posted teaching numbers that are the stuff of legend: 51 years in the classroom without missing a class, teaching well over a fourth of all the graduates in the history of the University. He will not be remembered for numbers, however, but for his message to us to keep on loving.

The people of the University are now grappling with a vision of its future. They are committed to a mission that flows from its Catholic, Marianist roots. They seek inspiration and imagination to inflame that vision with life.

Fifty years from now, when that vision has become history, a future generation may look at the deaths and retirements of its giants. We cannot predict who they will be nor the nature of their achievements. "God fulfills himself in many ways," said Tennyson's Arthur. But I have faith that those spiritual descendants of ours will have benefited deeply from Bombeck's and Burns' lessons of love and family. For, using an allusion many generations later than Tennyson, they have taught their children well.

A Death in the Family

The spring rains had stopped. On the first day of summer, the air was cool — a beautiful morning for a select soccer team to practice. My son Ben began to jog around the field to warm up. He collapsed. In minutes, he was dead.

No one knows why, 15 years and 50 days on this earth, his heart stopped beating. Cardiologists and coroners puzzle. Friends and family weep. And I cannot understand the mysteries of a God who could watch his own son die.

An aging Marianist writes me that we cannot understand why God gives us wonderful gifts — and that we cannot understand why he takes them away. Our pastor says he will pray but that he cannot help with the emptiness.

Scores praise Ben's life. "He was the best kind of kid," one parent says, "all parents pray to God their kids become." I hear of the unpopular student Ben did not fear to befriend. Several parents tell me how Ben welcomed their children when they were new to school or teams, even when Ben and they were feverishly competing with each other for playing time. One parent tells me that, when he grounded his son, Ben spent the day with him. A friend of Ben's says he once asked Ben if he feared death. He said "No." When asked why, he said that he felt that his faith was strong enough that when it came to be his time he would accept it and spend the rest of eternity with God in heaven.

I tell these stories to his soccer coach at Kettering Fairmont High School — where Ben received a varsity soccer letter his freshman year, played on the league champion freshman basketball team and earned A's in every subject except geometry, an advanced course whose teacher praised his hard work. The stories of faith and love bring me more tears than the lost promise of academic excellence and athletic grace. The coach says, "I wish, Tom, you could have seen him every day at practice. He was always like that."

People have trouble finding words to describe the spiritual qualities UD espouses or to say what it means to be a Catholic or to grow as an individual in a community. I wish they could ask Ben. For as one of his closest friends wrote on a card with flowers she sent, "Ben understands."

A BENCH BY BAUJAN

I sat on a bench, next to the walk behind Zehler Hall, overlooking Baujan Field. Before the soccer season wears down the grass, that broad expanse of green neatly lined in white has the perfection of an almost Platonic ideal of a soccer field.

I have found it and the Immaculate Conception Chapel both to be holy places to mourn for my son Benjamin, who died as summer began.

I can look at the goal area of the field and remember him, his grace and beauty. I can sense the workings of his mind. He is aware of all the players about him — offensive and defensive, the position of the ball and the possibilities of what to do with it. He played with an extraordinary sense of anticipation. Others inhaled his passion, his love of the game and of life.

That day on the bench at Baujan, I was feeling especially sorry at what I had lost. I had just come from the chapel. In its sanctuary, often lies open a book with pages labeled "Prayers Requested." The last handwritten entry looked like "*Gracias, Señor, por la vida.*" Ignorant of the language, I wondered whether someone was thanking the Lord for life in general or someone's in particular. I thought of Ben and, though thankful for what we had shared, felt little comfort.

I went to my bench by Baujan and continued to cry. As I sat with my head down, I sensed someone coming from my right. "If I keep my eyes straight ahead," I thought, "we won't disturb each other." As the person came near, a voice said, "Hi." I looked up into a smiling face. She continued walking, a young African-American woman wearing a green and white outfit with a dark blue backpack slung over one shoulder.

She wears the colors of Ben's soccer teams. In her eyes is Ben's welcoming love. Mystery. Incarnation. Christ in one another. The centuries search for words of explanation.

But words are just shadows of this smiling face and the laughter of my son.

Gracias.

'THIS PLACE IS DIFFERENT'

They were in Florence. To be surrounded by thousands of examples of the highest expression of the human spirit should have been heaven for two art historians. But art was not uppermost on the minds of Robin and Roger Crum.

"Where is he?" Roger asked with pain. "Just where is he?"

He was asking about John Howard, their son who had died at birth.

Robin's only reply: "He's watching."

Learned scholars can neither prove nor disprove her statement. I hope John Howard was watching when the Crums named their second son Raphael (literally, "God has healed") John. I hope he was watching when his father and I embraced and lamented our dead sons. I hope he was watching when his father told me of UD, "This place is different."

Roger knows it differs not because our faculty offices or Ghetto porches are different. It differs because of people who believe and hope and love.

One day as I skimmed a list-serve discussion by editors on the nature of higher education, I realized something of what makes UD people different — whether in class or on a porch, whether at home or at an alumni chapter's Christmas off Campus. Most schools limit the quest for truth largely to a search for hypotheses that can be validated, a worthy goal — but an approach to truth that cannot fully explain the spirit that created the art of Florence nor concern itself about whether John Howard watches.

A non-Catholic colleague told Roger that he liked teaching here because people believe deeply. "The academic and the spiritual coexist here," Roger told me, "and we don't have to explain it."

St. Paul encountered difficulty preaching Christ crucified to Greeks who sought wisdom. Here he has a place where people can seek both, a place where we may weep the deaths of our sons and we do not stand alone.

For those who love us are watching.

STRANGERS IN STRANGE LANDS

Alice Hengesbach sent me an e-mail. My memory reached back to 1950 to remember an Alice Hengesbach. She lived with Aunt Olive, my mother's aunt, far, far away on the east side of Cleveland. We lived west. A trip across town was a very big event. Alice and Olive's house was, it seemed, way out in the country. I recall they had a beautiful living room with early American furniture and a huge braided rug covering a wood floor. They were a branch of a big Hengesbach family tree, which one relative proudly traced back to a small German village.

The e-mail Alice is much younger. And she's much farther away than the east side of Cleveland. A member of the Peace Corps, she's teaching English to schoolchildren in Russia's Far East, beyond Siberia. She was asking fellow alumni for teaching aids to supplement outdated Communist textbooks.

A series of e-mail exchanges revealed I am also related to this younger Alice. Her great-grandfather is my mother's mother's brother.

As I looked at the photographs in this issue of German-Americans interned during World War II, I thought of generations of Hengesbachs. I thought of the Steigerwalds and the Branskys, relatives of Suzanne, my wife. I thought of our son, Ben, who ritually dressed for each major soccer match by donning beneath his jersey a tattered T-shirt emblazoned with the German national team's emblem: an eagle encircled by the words "Deutscher Fussball-Bund." I thought of how he and other youth — beneath their jerseys all "hyphenated" Americans by continent of ancestry — fantasized about proudly wearing the red, white and blue on a Afro-Asian-Euro-Hispanic...All-American team in competition with the rest of the world.

I thought also of the shame the internees carried for years. I thought of Dunbar's poetic rendering of the "face" he saw blacks forced to wear in a white society. I thought of fear and hatred and bigotry. And I thought of UD striving to be a community with diversity. Some say that's impossible. But, if we claim to follow the Christ who died for love, we have no other option.

THE GIFT OF GOD

Mary Beth, my sister, lives in Pittsburgh. While our children were growing up, we saw each other infrequently. Since my son Ben died, we have tried to be together more often. This summer we went on a vacation together. One day it rained all day. That was the day our mother died.

Her death was different from Ben's. She was 93. Strength had for years ebbed from her body and mind as my sister and the good people at the Villa de Marillac gave comfort to her age. Her death was not unexpected. But, in one way, the death of Gertrude Columbus was not unlike that of her grandson Benjamin. They were both inexplicable acts of God.

Mary Beth is a chemist. She seeks for reason and for cause. She sees death and wonders why the creator of the experiment of life, when he sees his creatures die, would not start over.

I remember a day in college when a teacher said that Ecclesiastes, a work I saw as beautiful, was incomprehensible to him because of its horror. I now feel that horror. I remember a few weeks ago when Don Donoher, in accepting the honor of having the Arena addition named for him, quoted from Ecclesiastes and noted its popularity at weddings and funerals. Many heard an honored coach, a perceptive teacher. I listened to a man whose son has died.

Ecclesiastes holds awesome beauty. I still find more truth there than in the concepts and the abstractions we use to define God and providence. But the closest view I have had of God was in the face of my son Ben as I realized his life was the result not only of the love of his mother and me, but also of the love of his sister and brother whose lives he emulated and of his friends and others who live in love. At weddings the weeks before and after my mother's death, I rejoiced at the hope of couples joined before a God of love.

But I still share Mary Beth's wonder at a God of love who can allow the pain of death. Ecclesiastes offers no hope of understanding: "No man can find out the work that God maketh from the beginning to the end." Perhaps that's why love is greater than hope or faith.

ON ERMA AND MARY

If there are typographical errors in the Erma Bombeck columns in this issue, we are sorry. It's hard to proofread with tears in your eyes.

My mother told me about Erma. I was a bright young thing, learning eagerly of Homer and Shakespeare. My mother told me I should read this columnist new to *The Plain Dealer*, Erma Bombeck. I did. My mother, like millions of other readers, was right.

Reading Erma's Christmas columns over and over again made me think of my mother. She was, as Erma observed of so many families, the one who took down the Christmas tree. She also, like other mothers, had a life known only obscurely by her children.

I knew she had, at the death of her father, dropped out of college after two years to help support her brothers and sister. I knew as a secretary at the old Cleveland Trust she had a respect for language that saved executives from embarrassment. I did not know, until after my father died and her mind had slipped into the shadows of age and I found her old college literary magazine, of her youthful ambitions to write.

Christmas Eve will soon be here, the saddest, drunkest night of the year, as my father — a career policeman — once told me, having sacrificed with my mother so that for me it was always among the happiest. But it is a night of much sorrow for those alone with crushed hopes, for those grown old, frail of body with minds slipping into the shadows, and for those who have lost those they loved and now grasp at emptiness.

Erma Bombeck accepted life's pain and sorrow and proclaimed with energy and laughter that we must grasp for something, for someone, because that is our human destiny.

I think maybe my mother realized years ago that Erma was like Mary, one who has seen the Truth. They saw Truth not in abstractions or formulations. They saw Truth as a child to hold in your arms or watch playing in the fields of Nazareth — or in the streets of the city or the back yards of suburbia.

WOULD JOE MAC LIE?

Joe McLaughlin told us we wouldn't have to go to meetings. He didn't exactly lie to Suzanne and me on that 1970s' day, but it might have dawned on us that an organization without any meetings would be a bit odd.

Joe — who in his too-short life did yeoman work in UD's sports, publicity, alumni and placement departments — knew his audience well. I had friends who had been in sodalities, fine groups but, to me, too close to institutions and "-isms" — objects of distrust. Joe knew we'd pray with him and his Family of Mary friends, but going to meetings was too much.

But, since he was a good man and he invited us, we joined and prayed and each got a nice medal. And nobody made us go to a meeting.

Over the years, a couple of Family of Mary groups did invite us to meetings. At one, a man believing strongly in the sacredness of life and the evil of abortion freely shared his view with that hatred and venom too-often attached to followers of the Prince of Peace. A young Marianist tactfully suggested compassion to unhearing ears. We left with admiration for the young Marianist and a reaffirmation of our dislike of meetings.

We went on with our lives, raising a family and pondering its joys in our hearts.

Then Ben, the youngest of that family, died. To help us survive, friends shared tears, brought casseroles and comfort and offered to help however they could. Judy and Tom Eggemeier, brave souls, asked us to go to a meeting. Since they are a good couple and they invited us, we went. We've been going to meetings of a Family of Mary group called Cana ever since.

As meetings go, I've been to worse. Wondering whether we should or could be doing something more significant, we come together and read the Sunday Scriptures and talk about them and pray and eat some food and drink some coffee and share much joy and sorrow.

What do we think of the Family of Mary now? They invited us to stand with them together before our God. They are good people.

IMPACT PLAYERS

Most of us go away to die. We grow old. We move. Or we fade so we are no longer recognizable. Even when the young die, they also usually die away from most of us — only a television or newspaper item disconcerts our routine.

Stacey Martin was one of the exceptions. She died in our midst. One moment she was on Baujan Field, exulting in the glorious game of soccer, playing with her teammates, watched by her parents. The next moment she lay dead.

She did not go away to die. Baujan, with its banners proclaiming the successes of our soccer teams, is at the center of our campus, near the chapel, drawing together academic buildings and student housing.

At a prayer service for Stacey Martin, the rector of the University, Father Gene Contadino, S.M., spoke of God as a coach. He spoke of the special relationship between coach and player. Each understands why the coach puts the player into a game or calls her to the sidelines. We, the crowd, do not.

While Father Gene spoke, I looked at the empty faces of Stacey Martin's teammates and saw again the empty faces of the teammates of my son Ben and thought: Stacey, Ben, Chris Daniels and so many others were not to us role players who gave us a few minutes or a few years. They were the impact players we need on the field and need in our lives.

We know we have a choice now. We can scream our hatred at a God who robs us. Or we can turn to each other, trying to see in each other a God of love as we saw that love in Stacey and Ben and Chris.

Sometimes empirical logic leads us inexorably to hatred or despair. But some experiences pierce the veil of seeming fact. On Ben's 17th birthday, as we sorrowed in his absence, we read a card from more than a dozen of his friends, thanking us for being his parents and raising him to be wonderful.

Although we do not understand our God, we hold in our hearts the wonder of Chris and Ben and Stacey. But we still must ask their inscrutable Coach, "How can we win without them?"

We are listening for an answer.

TIMELESS TRADITIONS

You never have the time, but sometimes you just take it.

Our paths on campus didn't cross when Don Donoher coached the Flyers. Our families didn't know each other. But when my son Ben died, Don and Sonia Donoher took time to pray, to send us a Mass card, connecting our families and unknown priests and God through the mysterious bond of prayer.

When I was young, I thought of achievement in terms of big accomplishments. I've learned that often it comes from the simple actions and frail gestures that weave the fabric of a life. When younger I left the private worlds of others alone. If I could not help, I should not intrude. When the Donohers grieved their son, I may have prayed, but I did not send a card. Perhaps I thought such a public figure would want to grieve in private. Perhaps I thought the gesture too frail. Perhaps I just didn't take the time.

I took a lot of time recently to write about the Donoher Basketball Center. We all knew something of Don Donoher as a teacher of basketball. We all learned more of his impact on others when John McHale, who once aspired to being a Flyer walk-on, gave $1.25 million for a building and told the University it should not bear his name but that of Don Donoher. And I learned more of the man when I called Rick Majerus. Hearing Donoher's name, Majerus, one of today's most successful basketball coaches, immediately took the time to tell me what a special person Donoher is and what a special place Dayton is.

It's a special place because the gestures, the time taken by Don Donoher and others have built into an achievement. *UDQ*'s article on the Donoher Center ends with coach Oliver Purnell — a coach who took time in mid-season to fly to Florida when a player was having an operation — talking about the Flyer spirit, about how young people here learn of team and community.

When Majerus says, "Dayton is now one of the premiere coaching jobs, and Don Donoher laid the foundation," he is talking about more than basketball.

He is talking about people who have taken the time.

THE BABY'S MAKING NOISE

Friends and relatives, we stand like a Greek chorus in the hospital hallway. Inside the room lies my daughter, Liz, attended by her husband, Tony, and a doctor. A cry. Megan Taylor Goheen is born. We do not know what to do. We applaud.

That day compresses all time to a single present moment.

I am a child of 10 sharing our front stoop with my mother, staring at the western stars.

I am a man, in idle conversation with my father about food, mentioning I don't like fried eggs crisp around the edges. "You mean I wasted all those years cooking you breakfast before school?" And I wish to take back the words and tell him I love crisp eggs and his uncritical love for me.

I am a husband and a father, and the 10-year-old Liz comes to Suzanne and me in bed to say the newborn Benjamin "is making noise."

She worried so. And now my mother and my father and my Benjamin are gone — beyond the stars, beyond our words, beyond our worries.

I worry now of Megan's newborn fragility and marvel at her strength and at the love of those who surround her. The love of parents and grandparents and friends. The love, for example, of her uncle Mike, our middle child, whose love brings him from Chicago to Megan's door five minutes after she arrives home and back there again two weeks later.

That weekend is that of All Saints and I think of the love of those the church calls triumphant. At Sunday dinner, "Aunt 'Reen" asks God's blessing and talks of Ben watching over us and praying for us.

Lying in the corner, Megan snorts. And the love at our table echoes a gathering in Bethlehem — far away in time but eternally present — to celebrate the birth of a baby who testifies eternally to the God of love dwelling within us. And each time I hold Megan or look at her, I know that the demons of hell and death, no matter their fierceness and their fury, shall not prevail against her.

What are we doing here?

'WRITE ABOUT MEGAN.'

That was advice Maureen Schlangen gave me when I admitted, as the other *UDQ* pages were on their way to the printer, that I had no idea what to put on this one.

But wouldn't that be the easy way out — for a grandfather to write about a beautiful granddaughter? She looked angelic at her baptism and so cute in the Arena in her "This is my first Dayton Flyers bib." (And I have pictures right here in my wallet.)

Reading about Megan would be a relief from a certain sadness that has dwelled in this space since Vol. 1, No. 1, when we reflected on the passing of Father Raymond Roesch, S.M., longtime UD president. But what does a recently baptized baby with her ears covered by her mother to soften the sound of thousands of fans in the UD Arena have to do with what UD is about?

Much.

It took an editor of a high-powered, multi-award-winning, beautifully produced magazine at a large state-supported university to point out to me what it is. Several years ago she had asked me why *UDQ* and a few other Catholic university periodicals stand out from most alumni publications, why we are able to deal with the issues we do in the way that we do. After our last issue, she gave me an answer. She wrote to say she was moved by the words appearing in this space; and, in searching for a label, she called them a prayer.

It's simple. At the University of Dayton, we can pray in print. We can speak of the transcendent, the spiritual. But, like many other people, our prayers surface mostly in times of sadness and of crisis or of dealing with "big" issues.

Perhaps they should surface at a laughing child, playing peek-a-boo with her blanket, at the pride of parents and the mystery of family, at the welcoming of a new member to what we call "community," to what we call "church," a community extending across barriers of place and time and bringing us together with a bond of eternal love. We should all write about our Megans.

A WALK IN THE PARK

Megan was going to take a walk in the park.

But she couldn't. The Klan was there.

So my 5-month-old granddaughter, her mother and grandmother did an Erma Bombeck kind of thing. They went to the mall.

I was left home with my curiosity, on the edge of Kettering's Lincoln Park, from which we often hear the sounds of concerts and other festivities. Today it was to be the sounds of hate. Kettering, with no law to prevent public rallies, braced for confrontation. Supporters of the Klan (actually some sort of branch of the group that once terrorized the country) were to number fewer than three dozen. But hundreds of protesters arrived, many bused in, many wanting to confront hate with hate and epithets and fists. We taxpayers were to spend $60,000 to keep these people from hurting each other.

Though curious, I did not take the short walk to gaze upon evil. Every person added made it more of an event that even reluctant news media would have to cover.

So I went across town to an event billed as Community Celebrating Diversity. The city, the schools and people of many faiths had decided to gather to show that a community can indeed celebrate diversity. As I arrived at an overflowing school gym, I looked around, saw lots of UD people and was glad. Community leaders spoke, and students from Fairmont and Alter and Colonel White sang. A Jewish cantor led us in "Let There Be Peace on Earth," and a youthful preacher exhorted us all to put our faith in Jesus.

Next to me a toddler sang "ba-ba-ba" in imitation of the singers and rolled her arms in response to the signer. When all applauded, the little girl joined in.

And I thought of Megan, who, when she is old enough to walk and sing and sign, will have a place and people to join because of these people, who, caring enough about the triumph of love over hate, did not just set aside their differences but gathered them up and brought them together and celebrated them.

CRAWLING TOWARD GOD

I thought it would be a good idea. A colleague had suggested that the writers of the publications group in the office all do stories on summer classes to be taught under the heading of "spirituality."

Of course, while the others were to be going to class, I was going to take a long-scheduled family vacation to ponder the mysteries of the sea, the un-numbered sands of the shore and the question of which restaurant to go to for dinner. No matter. I could read the books of the teacher, Jim Forest. And I could communicate with him by e-mail and, before vacation, interview him shortly after he came to campus from his home in the Netherlands.

When I arrived at the garden apartment serving as his temporary home, he offered to share with me his refrigerator's contents (that is, fruit juice or beer). In the midst of a hectic, hot summer, we sat and talked — of UD food service people he'd met who were discussing the Book of Revelation; of a gracious old woman in Atlanta with whom he had a long conversation about time and timelessness; of a possible mutual acquaintance, a religious woman who long served the church with her intellect and energy. Simply, we talked of the Incarnation, the God-made-man and his continued presence among us.

Such talk is not at the periphery of UD's mission. UD's vision proclaims that all truth is one, that the rigor of reason and the flights of faith are compatible. So not only does the religious studies department teach courses on spirituality, but also, for example, do the professional schools ask more questions, seek more connections, take more risks in expanding their visions than may be needed to train competent practitioners.

With the risk of moving beyond the known and the comfortable come criticism and, sometimes, failure. Without risk, failure is assured.

On vacation, I thought of this — not as I contemplated the sand and the surf — but as I watched my granddaughter learn to crawl. With laughter and energy, she burst forth toward a new, unknown world. And I grasped a little more of faith and reason and the incarnate love that makes them one.

LEADING US WHERE?

Thursday was a busy day that week. It was good to take a break to get to the Arena and see some basketball. In the middle of celebrating UD's birthday and kicking off a huge fund drive, one needs to consider the larger issues — like whether the Flyers will be able to outrebound opponents this year.

Thursday's opponents, Athletes in Action, provide exhibition games for college teams and make a halftime pitch for their particular take on Christianity, testifying to personal relationships with Jesus Christ. Their tone and emphasis on a direct line to God is not quite congruent with what many church-goers believe, but they are not afraid to bring Jesus into their daily lives.

UD's approach to God is more communal yet, at the same time, also intensely personal as we try to see God incarnate in one another.

That approach was evident in UD's daily life in the next day's *Flyer News*. A columnist had earlier written of the sudden death of the mother of a close friend. She raised questions of faith, writing, "I want to know how, after the death of a loved one, believing in God makes it easier to cope, grieve and try to regain the perspective of one who once saw meaning in the world."

In that Friday's issue, two sophomores tried to answer her questions. Both were eloquent in their belief in the triumph over death by God and by the good people they knew who had died. They both knew their words would not necessarily be persuasive. "Perhaps my logic is a little elementary," one wrote, "but in my opinion, death is such a profound experience that any logic would appear this way."

All three students profoundly loved those whom they lost. In sharing that pain in print both with friends and with those they've never met, in opening their souls to each other and to us, they've made a clear statement about the nature of what this University strives to be.

We know Jesus said, "Come, follow me." We wish he'd have been clearer about where he's leading us. But these students are showing us that the way is love. And let us hope and dare to believe that is also our destination.

'Go, UD! Go, Go, UD!'

"Megan, no whining."

Suzanne is instructing our granddaughter in the appropriate way to request a cracker, the 16-month-old's most consistently favorite food.

It's an instruction that is repetitive. But Megan usually comes to the realization that the assembly of sounds that are a natural and convenient way for her to ask for food are apparently not the words of choice for her parents and grandparents.

So she switches to a highly sibilant word, lacking any vowel sounds, but in her listeners' ears sufficiently similar to "please."

The cracker dialogue requires patience and love. It is a lot of effort to get to one word. But then the recently fruitful dialogue between Catholics and Lutherans about faith and good works took nearly half a millennium to yield one sentence. Working on this issue of *UDQ*, we encountered over and over again such dialogues, painful to begin, difficult to sustain, but ultimately bearing fruit.

UD's president spends years getting all the parties at the table so they can work together to better serve a community's children.

Although a school superintendent and a professor continually cut off phone conversations that become too heated to continue, they come back to talk more. And children will learn.

Christians and Jews, at odds for centuries, talk and talk and talk so that they might better worship their God, the one God in whom they each profess faith.

A man of faith and a man of reason come together to study. And they both learn of faith and reason and of how they learned what they have and of how far they have to go in learning more.

This all takes a lot of patience, humility, energy, time. We have to have the passion to care. We have to have the love to care about each other. We have to take the step of having civil words with each other. Then, sentences. Then as humans maybe we can make some progress. Perhaps that was what Megan was exhorting us to do when she spoke her first sentence, "Go, UD!"

WHERE THE ROAD GETS BAD

Aaron Priest was insistent. He wanted to be here in time for dinner. No matter that his plane was scheduled to land at 5:55 p.m. — after the guests were gathering in Kennedy Union for the dinner kicking off the Erma Bombeck Conference. I drew the assignment of picking him up at the airport.

I learned later that he had had a recurrent piece of advice for Erma, "Not to worry." But I worried. The road to the airport is a famous stretch of I-75. People from other parts of the country have an easy time placing Dayton. They remember, "That's where the road gets bad." So I left the office early that day, secured a parking space close to the terminal and waited.

The plane was late.

When finally free of the plane, Priest went with me to my car, well after the time many of Erma's other admirers were heading from the reception to the ballroom. I deduced his interest in getting here wasn't professional. It was personal. He was more than Erma's agent; he, like many coming to Dayton that day, was her friend. As we pulled into traffic, his talk moved quickly from the problems of the flight to an inquiry about the location of Woodland Cemetery, where Erma is buried.

To the dismay of some in Arizona, her home of many years, Erma's body is in Woodland because of its closeness to UD, to her childhood home and to the neighborhood where many years ago she met a boy named Bill.

The area must still have some charm. As we drove down I-75, the trucks parted and clear pavement appeared. We flew into Kennedy Union, up to the ballroom, to the table where Priest was to sit. It was full. But, "Not to worry." Bill Bombeck jumped up, embraced Priest and led him to his table. The next day he and the Bombeck family visited Woodland together.

Dinner. Death. Erma in life and beyond combines the ordinary and the transcendent. Priest, who controls approvals for Bombeck reprints, says that her serious columns are requested most. She was flippant and funny. But she knew where the road got bad. She'd been there. So we trusted her. We still do.

CARNIVAL AND CAPT. QUEEG

Several people said they liked the parrot on my hat.

In most places, a man in his mid-50s wearing a straw hat with a wooden parrot appended to it is an oddity. But this was in Cincinnati at a Jimmy Buffett concert, so I was less an oddity and more of the norm (though perhaps at the older end of the norm).

Some see Buffett as emblematic of hedonist escape. Some see Cincinnati as emblematic of censorship. Some people are always seeing something negative.

My parrot helps me see pleasant memories. Several years ago on another day in Cincinnati, Lianne DeBanto Massa '92 (a housemate then of my daughter, Liz) gave it to me. At the concert that year, Lianne looked over at Liz and her parents and her brothers and exclaimed, "They all know the words!"

To me, they are words that sometimes have a peculiar, personal resonance. For example, the Buffett musical, *Don't Stop the Carnival*, is based on a book by Herman Wouk, writer also of *The Caine Mutiny*, upon whose central moral issue of authority and responsibility I wrote my first serious essay in high school.

Some prefer to dismiss any moral message from a man who makes millions from many who drink too much to hear his music, let alone listen to any message. Others may scoff at Cincinnati, seeing it as the town that censored the work of Robert Mapplethorpe.

And some don't like Catholics because they see them as slighting women. And Jews and Arabs, blacks and whites, Democrats and Republicans can find all sorts of reasons — many of them solid — for not wanting to listen to each other.

Locally, I volunteer for United Way. Some people don't like United Way because it funded a Boy Scout program. Others don't like United Way because they think it gives too little to the Boy Scouts.

We can find reasons to shun working with any person or any group.

UD, fortunately, is still a place where people, even if they don't agree with you, will listen to you and talk with you, even if you're from Cincinnati or have a parrot on your head.

A FIRE ONE EVENING

The game was over. Kettering Fairmont had beaten Centerville for the high school boys' district soccer title, the first time ever the Firebirds had beaten the Elks. As the crowd dispersed, Suzanne and I helped get Megan into Liz's car, waved goodbye to granddaughter and daughter and walked slowly back to where we had parked.

On the way, we ran into a couple we knew. "We're having a few people over for a fire in our backyard," they said. "Come over." We did. It was like old home week. Most of those there were parents of teammates of our son Ben, when he was a youth player and for the year he played for Fairmont before he died.

The parents talked of things that parents talk of. Some had just attended UD's Parents Weekend. They spoke of the hot tub two of their sons had installed on their UD porch, of its removal called for by University officials, of joy in their children and worries. They spoke of one son whom parents on the sidelines years earlier sometimes confused with Ben — both blond and fast, running with their spines straight and burning with competitive zeal. Was he now going to apply himself zealously to his studies, his mother wondered. At Parents Weekend, other engineering students came to him with questions. Had he paid them to do so to impress mom?

A late arrival came from the team victory party. He had a son finishing a glorious high school soccer career. For seven years, as a proud father he'd followed his sons playing Fairmont varsity soccer. So, too, might have I, three with Mike, and four with Ben — had he lived. I thought of what was not, but there were then no tears. Instead, I rejoiced by that fire in the joy of these parents and their sons and of those in Centerville against whom they had played that night and of all their energy and joy and love of the game and of life. Those were things that mattered to Ben.

Meanwhile at home, Megan in bed, Liz was e-mailing me a copy of a poem her husband's aunt had given her. It begins, "When tomorrow starts without me … I wish so much you wouldn't cry." And it spoke of God's love.

When I read it, of course I cried. But the tears, I hope, reflected the fire of a spirit that burns in families and among those who gather in the evening to speak of those they love.

IT'S ABOUT TIME

We stood, some in the evening drizzle, some dry beneath the overhang above the Kennedy Union steps. About 200 of us, we stared at the clock face on the Miriam Hall tower. As the clock struck seven, the show began. We saw and heard, first, words — geological and literary — about time, then hearts pounding and blood pulsing, cars and people traveling, breathing long and labored. …

I tried to put into words my reaction to this student-and-faculty event, part of It's About Time, an assignment for all visual arts students. As close as I could get that evening was, "I don't know what I like, but I know art." This — in its energy, its allusion, its strength — was art.

The next day I took time to view the displayed student efforts. Hallways and classrooms and studios held an explosion of creativity. Some were clever. Some were bold. Some forced thought. One was troubling — a wall plastered with death certificates, of many yet to die. To view this, I had interrupted editing obituaries of B.J. Bedard, the man who hired me at UD, and Joe Stander, a man well suited to be a trustworthy administrator because he'd really rather be fishing. I had recently shared wordless sorrow with friends at the death of their son. And I was soon to learn of the death of an aged priest, Bud Horst, who had baptized our oldest children and to the dismay of some of his religious brothers many years ago would invite his friends, including a woman (my wife, Suzanne) to share post-bowling refreshment with him in Alumni Hall. We all react personally to art. I am reacting as one also experiencing vivid reminders that time is something we're just passing through.

I write this, having just come from Sunday Mass, where looking down at my 2-year-old granddaughter Megan content with her rag doll, I heard choir and congregation proclaim, "Glory to God in the highest and peace to his people on earth." Daunting and seemingly impossible tasks for those just passing through time.

Memories of the past persist. A skilled department chair. A shy provost. A crusty priest embracing change. Friends. Children. Visions of a future rise. A young girl in church calls a stuffed piece of cloth, "My baby."

Confronting what is daunting. Attempting what seems impossible. That is what this church existing in time does. And, apparently, we are called to do it, too.

For the church is us.

STEP BY STEP

Mary's e-mails from France are happier now.

When Mary Harvan Gorgette's son, David, was born, he was very tiny. Doctors debated how to treat him. Mary's friends here prayed for him, for her, for her husband, Frédéric.

Mary worked in this office while a student at UD. After graduation in 1991, before gaining a Ph.D. in Texas, she lived in Sierra Leone, learning much and loving its people. She wrote about them for *UDQ*. We were somewhat guiltily glad that now she was not there and David was being cared for in the hospitals of Paris.

But we also know how the best of parents, the best of intentions, the best of medical care can all be often not enough. Later in these pages — from Plaza through Class Notes — there are stories of UD people confronting death. They are intertwined with announcements of birth and stories of the struggles in between. We work for a part of the University that's entrusted to raise money for programs and facilities. But those programs and facilities are for people who are encountering birth and death and the space in between.

I'm reminded of a similar fact as a local United Way committee I serve on meets to distribute funds for programs serving area young people. Requests to fund programs for youth services far exceed our ability to raise money. With God's grace, we will try to fund the best, the most effective. But good and effective programs will go without. And people — like the children of mothers who have worked their way off welfare but can't afford decent day care — will go without.

Some people look at budgets of billions and try to build programs to help. State legislators in Ohio are now struggling to balance human services needs with all the other priorities of the state. And revisions may have to be made as federal decisions are made.

Others take smaller steps. Students in UD's Habitat for Humanity chapter built a house this year. A few more UD students each year teach in urban schools.

Meanwhile in France, nurtured by parents and prayer and grace, David Gorgette has grown ounce by ounce into a healthy baby. Maybe that's how it has to be done — whether with babies or houses. Ounce by ounce. Nail by nail. Student by student.

DO WE WANT AN ANSWER?

I'd rather be writing about Megan.

I could write about how, when her father comes home from work, she hides, and her mother — my firstborn — asks, "Where's Megan?" and Daddy looks for her. And how the other night in the park, playing a partially learned game of hide-and-seek, Megan leaned against a pine, put her forearm over her eyes and said, "Where's me?"

But, looking at the issues covered in this *Quarterly*, it's hard to write about Megan. We have recorded a lot of controversy here: President Bush and stem cells, Boy Scouts and homosexuals, awards and those who object to those receiving them, sacred places and profane tourists, a Church potentially divided by the calls of faith and reason.

That is not a pleasant prospect for a 2-year-old about to turn 3.

Meanwhile, her grandfather tries to chronicle a world in which a desire for the comfort of healing not only blurs for some their vision of where life begins but also obscures the value of life itself, a world where the zeal of the righteous can ignite the hatred of intolerance.

To one not sure how hide-and-seek is played, I cannot explain a desire to heal that kills, a desire to love that hates. I need to tell her stories of those who move beyond the hate and the destruction.

Perhaps someday I can find a way to tell her the story of the archbishop and the theologian. In these pages, the theologian writes of something called *mandatum*, about which Megan and others care little. But the real story is of two men who love their Church, who came together to the table in the name of Christ and talked. Though they don't know what the future holds, they know enough to pray together in the Church of Christ for that future and for us.

Perhaps we all could pray and beneath a tree, like Megan, ask, "Where's me?"

Perhaps we should stop and listen for an answer.

Perhaps we might hear the Holy Spirit speaking softly in the breeze.

FEAR AND UNCERTAINTY

Megan calls me "Papa." It's not because she can't say, "Grandpa." Sometimes she speaks profoundly.

On Sept. 11, she said, "Fire burns. It hurts people."

She had just seen a television replay of jet fuel at the World Trade Center bursting into flames. I had hoped that she, then not yet 3, was still immune from the terror of reality. Perhaps she was, but her words indicated that innocence is ephemeral.

Suzanne and I had come home that afternoon wanting to be with our children and grandchild. Before going to Megan's, we talked by phone to our son Mike, who in the midst of a three-year return to Dayton for law school lives but a few blocks away. As we spoke, both our houses shook at the loud crash of two closely spaced explosions. A logical explanation, one later supplied by news media, was that the noises were sonic booms.

But sonic booms had long since been banished from our neighborhood; pilots respected the tranquility of urban residents. Today, we knew was different. We knew the president was returning to Washington. A direct flight path would pass near Dayton. A television station reported a plane crash and showed, from a traffic cam, smoke in the distance. We saw in the sky a vapor trail suddenly ending. Fear and uncertainty had spread throughout the country.

I suppose that's how people felt in 1941 as they scanned our coasts for the invasion that never came. Perhaps it's what some adults felt in our old neighborhood in the 1950s as we lived near a missile site protecting us from a bombardment that never came. Now we have been attacked. Now we have to respond.

As Megan went off to bed on Sept. 11, she made a point of articulating her feelings: "I love gama. I love papa. I love daddy. I love mama. I love everybody."

Perhaps it is time for those of us surrounded by love to use it to shape the world.

WALKING AN UNKNOWN PATH

I've been at UD for parts of five decades. I know where all the buildings are. They've changed over the years, but the president's name has always been Ray. And the Cincinnati Province of the Marianists has always been in Dayton.

It's a world we've gotten used to. And now it's about to change. Four provinces of Marianists are combining their headquarters in St. Louis, and Brother Ray Fitz will be leaving the presidency.

In late January, an overflow crowd in a room in Kennedy Union listened to Brother Stephen Glodek, S.M., who will be the provincial of the new Province of the United States of the Society of Mary, speak on "The Marianists' Commitment to UD." Like many leaders, he spoke of change and challenge. Unlike many, he cast his thoughts in scriptural terms, using the story of the road to Emmaus. The disciples were confused. What many had expected had not come to pass. The future was uncertain. Yet they were walking with Christ. But they did not recognize him until they broke bread together.

Glodek's talk came to mind on a recent Sunday as I attended a Mass at which Archbishop Daniel Pilarczyk presided over the sacrament of confirmation. His humor and intellect reminded me of seeing him at a meeting with UD's religious studies faculty. Bishop and theologians, they had in prayerful and respectful community looked at a future none can predict. I was also reminded of his simple and clear advice to UD's trustees, "You have been given charge of a complex and delicate community, a community that involves both the saving providence of God and the greatest achievements of humanity … don't mess it up."

These mental wanderings came into focus as I saw returning to their pew from the bishop's anointing a recently confirmed young man and his sponsor, his sister. Years ago she had dated my younger son, who had wrestled and played with her younger brother, then a child, now become a man in Christ. Returning to their pew, brother and sister smiled broadly at each other. Years of memories of family and friends and fear and love suddenly flowed over me.

I then realized the choir was humming a tune whose title came to my mind in the terms of my youth: "Come, Holy Ghost."

WHERE IS THE FACE OF GOD?

"Come, Holy Ghost" were the last three words in this space three months ago. Those just confirmed and Marianists forming a new province were looking for guidance for their futures. But that wasn't front-page news of the sort that is now sending a whole church to ask the Spirit to be present.

Jesus has left us. He promised to send us the Holy Spirit. That's the material of the liturgy this time of year. Where do we find this Spirit? Some 90 percent of Americans believe in God. But they turn their backs on the churches and look for spirituality within. That some church leaders concern themselves more with scandal and notoriety than with sin and contrition may not help Americans move beyond their individuality.

Institutions are fallible. So it's just me and Jesus.

Except that's not the message of Jesus.

God became man to save me. That's true. But he did so to save you, too. The Incarnation brings us together for eternity.

But in a world of sin and condemnation, of accusation and of refusal to accept responsibility, where is this Jesus who has risen? The disciples on the road to Emmaus didn't recognize him until they broke bread with him. When he ascended, his companions stared into the sky until two men in white garments asked them why they stood there staring.

Then, at Pentecost, the Spirit came with a driving wind and tongues of fire. Where will we find the Spirit? Perhaps we could look for inspiration at the lives of a century-and-a-half of Marianists who are commemorated in this issue. Or maybe we can look at the celebrations for the decades of Brother Fitz's presidency. Maybe we can look at the just-completed campus conversations on our Catholic, Marianist identity that have led to reflections on our past and visions of our future.

Maybe we should look at each other — at the thousands of alumni whose lives are chronicled in class notes, at our families, at our co-workers, at the sinners and the saved. Maybe we should look at each other, because, through the mystery of the Incarnation, in each others' faces we see the face of God. It is our beginning and our end.

ALL THINGS TRITE AND BEAUTIFUL

"What's a cliché?" I heard Joe Pici of the English department pose that question decades ago. I still wonder with what degree of ironic perversity it was meant. A writer who can make us smile and cry, Joe knows how to avoid what is trite, what is worn out by constant use, what is no longer fresh. But he also knows that, since before Homer, crafters of tales have told the same stories of birth and life and death, of fear and hope.

Vol. 1, No. 1, of *UDQ* contained an editor's column because, since we could not afford a full-fledged design, Page 2 was blank. Colleagues told the editor to write a column. I did not know what to write. Then Father Roesch died, and I wrote of priests six deep at his funeral and of the congregation singing "Amazing Grace." Through the years I've written more words of deaths: Tom Frericks, Chris Daniels, Ben Columbus. And words of births. And of lives. And always of amazing grace.

The plot of birth-life-death may be worn out by constant use, but what may be clichés can also fire our spirits. Memories of friends, of houses with creaky porches. Weddings bringing together not just man and woman but friends who, gone from Dayton, still have a spirit of place and perhaps of eternity in their hearts.

As each school year begins, an extraordinary newness rumbles through lives — new faculty, always new students, this year a new president. It's all happened before, of course. Most things have.

Certainly many old editors have become grandfathers for the second time. It's happened over and over. But only one old editor has looked into the face of this feisty little redhead called Molly and seen all that's gone before on Earth renewed. And each of you who reads this has been the only one at one particular moment who looked at a single other person — a friend, a spouse, a parent, a child — and seen a glimpse of eternity.

Life has infinite sadness and painful beauty, but all moves beyond triteness when one human can look at another and snatch a darkling vision of eternal joy.

WRITING ABOUT BENEFITS

The cost of our health-care benefits is going up. Everybody's is. But besides paying for mine, I'm paid to write about them. I was going to do so before I left for dinner.

But late that afternoon my daughter and her husband were closing on a new mortgage. Suzanne asked if I wanted to go with her to pick up our granddaughters at nursery school.

I weighed that offer against continuing to wrestle with the best way of telling colleagues that, although we have pretty good benefits and the University pays a higher percentage than most employers do, we were going, right after Christmas, to pay a good amount more ourselves.

Somehow I decided to put writing aside until after dinner and go spend some time with Megan and Molly.

We went first to Molly's daycare room. Standing across the room on the legs of an 11-month-old, she pointed to us, decided she couldn't walk yet and crawled over to us, stopping only briefly to play with a ball on the floor.

Then we gathered 4-year-old Megan and her belongings. I noted with grandfatherly pride the sophistication of her drawings. She told us of her field trip. The farm had a swamp and was "stinky."

After picking them up, Suzanne and I went to the park. While Suzanne and Megan played on the slide, I pushed Molly on a swing. She laughed.

As the waning day's chill hit the air, we went back to our house. Suzanne fed Molly and suggested I look for an old set of blocks to amuse Megan. We thought they were stored in the "study," a room with a computer, family photographs, vinyl records, fading books and old toys.

Megan asked, "Was this Uncle Ben's room?"

My son Ben died at the age of 15, more than two years before Megan was born.

"No," I said, "his room was upstairs. But I keep some of his things here."

"He's in heaven now," Megan told me.

■ ■ ■

Some people ask what stories like this have to do with UD.
Everything, I think.
Or why do people come here?

LIGHT IN WINTER

During World War I, a Catholic priest served as a stretcher bearer, carrying wounded Muslim soldiers to safety and comforting the dying. One moon-filled night, he had a vision about the connected nature of creation. Pierre Teilhard de Chardin survived the trenches, then lived to write a number of philosophical and religious works. His religious superiors refused to let him publish them in his lifetime. He obeyed.

We serve our God in many different ways.

Ursula King has spent her life becoming the world's greatest scholar of those works. The University of Dayton recently gave her an honorary degree. While on campus, she participated in a religious studies seminar and in the opening of the UD women's center.

We serve our God in many different ways.

In the gray Ohio winter, the people of my town perform small acts of kindness, helping with stalled cars and shoveling each other's snow. And they try to fill the shrinking pantries for the hungry and worry about the overflowing shelters for those cold and homeless.

We serve our God in many different ways.

Colleagues of a faculty member stranded in a foreign country after Christmas covered his classes without complaint. As winter lengthens, our students read their books and write their papers and ponder war and peace. They wonder how and when to act.

We serve our God in many different ways.

In these cold months, Marianists — to show their spirit and promote UD's nature — hang banners, hold games, give awards and sponsor lectures. And they pray.

We serve our God in many different ways.

And, in this winter of cold and fearful anticipation, granddaughter Molly went, accompanied by Mama and sister Megan, for her 15-month checkup. Molly was quiet and unimpressed with the nurse's stethoscope. To overcome the child's reticence, the nurse asked, "Can you dance, Molly?" Molly did not respond. But 4-year-old Megan knew that, if she sang, her sister would dance. So the grown-ups asked her to sing. She sang, not the expected "Twinkle" or "Ring-Around-the-Rosie."

Megan sang "Amazing Grace."

And Molly danced.

And we all serve God in many different ways.

RESTLESS

Mike was born restless. Once our middle child was big enough to get up on his hands and knees, he would rock back and forth, bouncing himself to sleep. Restless in school, he was fortunate to have teachers who saw this as a gift not a handicap.

He majored in chemistry at UD, spent some time at a marine research and educational facility on Big Pine Key, traveled the small towns of the country in a business job unrelated to science, moved to Chicago and into information technology. Three years ago, he started law school, choosing Dayton over several other possibilities.

This spring he graduated.

He's the one in the family I don't write about much. His sister, the teacher, has a quotable 4-year-old and a cute toddler. His mother has lived with me for 37 years. His brother died a teenager. Words about them come easier. It's harder to write about the restless.

I knew he had grown up and gotten really smart when, some years back, my seemingly unsentimental and skeptical son gave me a gift — a rendering of the two of us on a park bench with the Mark Twain quotation: "When I was a boy of 14, my father was so ignorant I could hardly stand to have the old man around. But when I got to be 21, I was astonished at how much the old man had learned in seven years."

I consider it prudent not to ask what he thinks at 31.

With a UD law degree, there is no doubt that he thinks like a lawyer. And, after studying for and taking the bar exam, he will work like a lawyer. What will that mean?

For parents of college-age children, that often means will he get a job, what kind, where?

For some of us, those are now not among the most important questions. The important ones are more nebulous. The Family of Mary group to which Mike's mother and I belong is at a point of trying to formulate some of those. Who are we? What should we be doing? We should have some guidance; since the name of the group is Cana, we will do whatever He tells us — as soon as we discern what that is.

What will Mike do? Join a law firm, start his own, get a Ph.D. in a scientific field? I don't know. I do know that the day after graduation was Mother's Day and he brought his mother a dozen roses. He may be restless, but he's smart.

FROM ALUMNI TO KU

He was one of the old brothers that students for decades have seen trudge from Alumni Hall to Kennedy Union. He often ate lunch at the Kennedy Union Food Court. On Aug. 1, Brother Edward Prochaska, S.M., in the 10th decade of his life, sat down with friends for lunch in the KU Food Court, put his head down on the table and died.

People tried feverishly to revive him; workers were troubled going back to their jobs. This I heard from a colleague who asked me about the procedure for announcing deaths on campus, now that the Marianist provincial headquarters is no longer in Dayton. I suggested she ask Father Gene Contadino, S.M., a liaison between the Marianists and the University and, from time to time, one of Brother Ed's lunch partners.

She returned from talking to Father Gene with a different image of Brother Ed's dying — one not of commotion and fear but of a 92-year-old man who was ready to die having lived a full life.

A few days later, I talked with Gene about Brother Ed and his dying. "It was sad," he said. "But it wasn't bad." Ed's life touched others. To the son of a co-worker, he was a great shooter-of-rubber bands. To colleagues, he was a turner-off-of-lights and lecturer-on-saving-electricity. To many, he was a laugher-to-make-you-not-take-yourself-so-seriously.

Though his health was declining, Gene said, "You never heard him complain. That's the old brothers; they wouldn't tell you."

He was old school in many ways. Although his religious order and his University had a global reach, Ed's life went from Alumni Hall, where he slept, to Zehler Hall, where he worked at UD Printing and Design, to Kennedy Union, where he ate, and back to Alumni.

"Many people say, 'I have to go there, do that, accomplish this.' But Ed was not driven. He didn't have to go somewhere," Gene said.

His life was a testimony, Gene said, to a reality that "just because you're retired and you don't travel the world or even the city, you can have a tremendous impact on people."

"He was like the grandfather that you'd love to have in your house," Gene said. "You didn't have to cater to him. He told stories. He fed you more than you fed him."

A large number of people came to the funeral of a 92-year-old man whose life was circumscribed by Alumni Hall, Zehler Hall and Kennedy Union because, Gene said, "when he touched somebody, it counted."

DO THEY LISTEN?

Children can convince us that the Incarnation is not an abstraction.

Suzanne and I usually attend the 9:30 a.m. Sunday Mass at our parish. On All Souls Day, however, I found myself, in the Immaculate Conception Chapel after the 10 a.m. Mass, trying to explain death and resurrection to 5-year-old Megan. Her sister had brought us to that point. After the previous evening's dinner, Molly, not then 2, had quietly announced, "I sleep at grandma's house." Grandma could not turn down the request.

Grandma and grandpa, however, were not swift enough to dress and feed Megan and Molly in time for 9:30. We arrived at the chapel just in time to beat Father Jim Heft inside the door. The only four seats together were in the front row. Fortunately we had crayons; Megan's careful rendering of windows and crosses hangs now in my office.

As the children drew, the congregation dwelt on death. At the chapel's side altars, memorials for the Days of the Dead, as All Saints and All Souls days are known in Mexico, commemorated those who died attempting to cross desert regions to life in the United States. The memorials presented words of Isaiah, "They will neither hunger nor thirst, nor will the desert heat beat upon them."

Father Heft's homily spoke of the sudden death of his father. I pondered the sudden death of my youngest child. Father Heft spoke of Aquinas' speculation on the forms our bodies take once they are resurrected. Stories I'd heard of the kindness of my dead son led to images of him somehow easing the pain of the children who died in the desert.

As I talked to Megan after Mass, I tried to translate the day's complexity of scripture and theology to a 5-year-old's level. I assumed that, although she was quiet in church, she could not have been listening. So I said to her that today's Mass was about people who had died and gone to heaven.

"But they didn't mention Uncle Ben," she said. She had been listening. And she had put death in the context that it exists — that of the individual person. I pray she grows to love the individual person, Jesus, God incarnate, who for us triumphs over death.

She is listening.

And in our churches and our houses, in our cities and our deserts, all the children of the world may be listening.

WHO KILLED CHRIST?

I know who killed Jesus.

I did.

That's what the sisters told me when I was a child. The thorns, the whips, the nails that pierced his flesh were my sins.

Those women may have had a really negative attitude, but we did learn to avoid near occasions of sin, bad companions and a whole lot of other stuff.

Somehow we may have also learned to avoid anything tainted in the world. So we can avoid the Democratic Party because we object to its stand on abortion. We can avoid Republicans because we don't see them committed to social justice. We don't give to organized charity because we don't trust institutions. We shun our church because we've seen its leaders to be sometimes flawed.

I find myself sometimes vexed that I cannot convince others to forgive some of the human failings of institutions and to value more the organized capacity of a community to care for itself. This vexation can become acute around Christmas as it did one day this December. That evening I was to attend a party with UD colleagues in Oakwood (old money). In the afternoon a United Way committee I serve on was visiting three agencies in neighborhoods across the river (old poverty).

But hope and insight spring unexpectedly. At the first agency we visited, children were eagerly awaiting a visit from UD basketball players. At the second, staff praised the capable help of UD students. The third, though with no UD connection, had the stable support of a Protestant church, which reminded me of the large local impact of church agencies, particularly Catholic Social Services. At that third youth center, a young man was asked how he had changed over the years there. He smiled and said, "People tell me I used to be a piece of work."

He was still a piece of work; now serving as a mentor to young children and as a spokesman for his community, he was doing more than avoiding evil.

He and those who helped him were doing more than avoiding adding their sins to the Crucifixion. As Christians we might say that, made in the image and likeness of his God, the young man was, perhaps as the good sisters of my youth were, accepting and sharing the grace of the Risen Lord.

A TASTE OF BROCCOLI

In art and liturgy and life, we have had much of suffering and death lately. And, in Dayton, we have had much of rain.

One recent day the rain came hard and heavy. And suddenly it stopped. The sun shone. A rainbow? My wife and I went out our front door and looked. And there it was. We called our daughter's family. Our son-in-law listened to aging, silly grandparents relate the news of color in the eastern sky.

The next day we learned he showed our granddaughters, from their front door, the rainbow. He told them it looked as though it came to earth near their church, named for the great reformer St. Charles Borromeo. And, for they share in an Irish heritage, he told them of leprechauns and pots of gold at the end of the rainbows. And so they sought the end of the rainbow. But it faded and no gold was found — until they returned home, where somehow golden-covered chocolate coins had found their way beneath the girls' pillows.

So let us now, in the midst of suffering, praise the God of rainbows who gives hope in suffering and dandelions in spring so children may pick them and have abundant gifts for elders whose eyes have dimmed to the beauty of creation.

Let us open our eyes and look around for gifts so numerous we have not seen them —

Let us give thanks for ice cream, for it makes the cow a noble animal.

Let us give thanks for broccoli, for parents can tell children to try something, it's good for them.

Let us give thanks for the children who try the broccoli and those fewer who like it, for that brings much rejoicing among mothers.

Let us give thanks for cats sleeping in the sun, for even the Lord of Creation rested.

Let us give thanks for dogs barking at unseen rabbits, for we all must contemplate the unseen.

Let us give thanks for birds chirping an hour before dawn, for they announce the lifting of the darkness.

Let us give thanks and praise the God of Abraham and Noah for the awesome gift of creation and for our humbling task of stewardship, for the Resurrected Lord and for rainbows come to earth.

THE GRAY HAT

Through the fog of memory, I recall a blue cap and a gray one, gifts perhaps of my grandmother. The blue was battered but beloved. The gray remained looking always new. It was never worn.

I was urged to wear it. It looked much better than the faded, worn blue one. I was unable to articulate why I could not wear an emblem of the enemies of our Union, promoters of slavery, slayers of the young soldiers defending the Republic.

It probably didn't take much arguing to avoid wearing the hat. In those days in Cleveland, Ohio, most anything south of the Ohio Turnpike was suspect.

Many years later, those memories came back to me when, watching the Ken Burns' documentary of the Civil War, I heard the words of a Tennessee man fighting there for the Confederacy. He was asked, I think by Union soldiers, why he was fighting. He was not rich. He didn't grow cotton. He didn't have slaves. He had little in common with those who did and might benefit from this war. So why did he fight?

"Because you're on my land," he replied.

Today we seem to all be on each other's land. Whether in politics or religion or in looking for a parking space, somebody else's solution seems to be my problem, and I've got a good notion to give him a piece of my mind. But then, minds, with a decline in reading and conversation and civility, don't seem to be as useful as they once were.

One political pundit has suggested that the current tension among those who are passionately reviving the tensions of the Vietnam War will only subside when those of us who then lived in this country are dead. The tensions of the Civil War lasted as long as the lives as those who experienced it — if not longer.

Does every major tension have to wait until we die to be dissolved? No wonder some of our Christian brothers and sisters so eagerly await Armageddon.

The times bring back another childhood memory — of images in books of a man with a sad, tired face who told his country: "With malice toward none, with charity for all, with firmness in the right as God gives us to see the right, let us strive on to finish the work we are in, to bind up the nation's wounds. …"

GLORY AND PRAISE

On a sunlit September morning, I looked forward to a full day — a lingering cup of coffee, a slow amble around the duck pond, the leisurely reading of a book. Those were my thoughts until my wife and daughter mentioned that granddaughter Megan was spending the day with a friend, mother and grandmother would love to go shopping and how'd I like to spend the day with 2-year-old Molly.

After gobbling down her Golden Nugget breakfast, Molly was excited about going to a "special place." I had thought some suspense about an unknown destination might keep her interest. But as she guessed that we might be visiting the Magic Castle or a fall festival, I began to have my doubts that driving down the road to Carillon Park and its lessons in history would hold the toddler's interest.

But they did. Docents spoke to her directly of the wonders of the Wright brothers and one-room schoolhouses. The trains presented such a treat we did them twice. When she wanted to see the "little house" again, I marveled at her interest in Newcom's Tavern, Dayton's oldest building. But what she meant by a little house was a child's playhouse behind the tavern.

Children see things differently. She did not see my feelings, I think, when I noticed her next to the park's flag pole — she in her red-white-and-blue Fourth of July dress echoing the colors of the flag at half-staff, for it was Sept. 11.

She did not as the day ended listen as I did to CNN recalling the horrors of that day, now years ago but ever-present. The reporter's voice broke but once, as she spoke of a kindergarten being evacuated, the second plane hitting and a child turning to her father with a newfound horrible knowledge: "Daddy, they're doing it on purpose."

All this remained in my mind Sunday morning in the Chapel of the Immaculate Conception as UD's special events choir assembled to sing with a visiting writer of holy songs, as the congregation listened to the reading of the Prodigal Son and pondered sin and grace, as we prayed to the God of Abraham, "All glory and praise be yours, O God. … With faith and hope and love, we sing Amen."

And I saw behind the choir in the old sanctuary the morning sun streaming through the rosette window of Christ crucified.

CLASS NOTES

"Amazing grace" were the first words printed in this space when *UDQ* took its present format in 1991. The budget for the re-design of the publication didn't cover this page. The death of Father Raymond A. Roesch, S.M., longtime president of UD, made clear, however, that the subject matter would be a reflection on the man remembered as the architect of UD as a major university. The theme of grace has remained a constant in these Page 2 vignettes, which have through narratives of specific instances tried to show that grace is indeed amazing, that through our fellow beings we can gain a glimpse of God.

Since you last received *UDQ*, the community that is the University of Dayton has seen more of the immutable parade of death — Hebeler, King, Ruff, Sears, Yano and countless others among the tens of thousands connected by the bonds of this institution. Reflecting on the lives of those who have left us can bring us closer to our God.

But so, perhaps, can a less sorrowful activity, a reading of what some who know not better see as banal — class notes.

University of Dayton alumni have connected themselves — through living and learning together, through their fun and their faith — in an extraordinary way. This issue of *UDQ* presents measurable evidence of that. An October edition of our e-mail supplement, *New from UDQ*, noted a decline in the volume of class notes in the most recent *UDQ* and light-heartedly pointed out that the 1970s were in danger of moving from being labeled as individual years to being lumped together as a decade like the 1960s and 1950s. Our hope was to move the 15,000-word winter volume of class notes closer to the previous issue's volume of 22,000 words.

This spring issue contains class notes totaling 36,000 words. The 1970s have year-by-year headings. And so again do the 1960s. Tens of thousands of words of sharing news of births and deaths, jobs and children, sufferings and joys, meeting old friends and missing them — it's the stuff of everyday life and of eternity, of sadness and of joy.

Recently, Father Norbert Burns, S.M, in his 81st year of life and seventh decade of teaching, was speaking to a campus audience about relationships. He pointed to a crucifix on the wall. He said to look beyond the suffering to the joy, to the open tomb of Easter.

So as you rekindle relationships with old Flyer friends, be joyful. You have been blessed with an amazing grace.

12:05 MASS

Introibo ad altare dei.

Ad deum qui laetificat juventutum meum.

"I will go to the altar of God."

"To God who gives joy to my youth."

Occasionally I recall the Latin of my youth, the words of the priest, the response of the server. Sometimes it's stress or daydreaming or just the random connections of an aging brain. At the 12:05 Mass one recent day, it was stress. Suzanne, my wife, was going to have surgery.

Te rogamus.

So I was praying as a supplicant. Of the four kinds of prayer — adoration, contrition, supplication and thanksgiving — one that has always been a big hit is the kind that asks God for something. On our knees, in the book of intentions of our parish, in bed during a wakeful night, we pray in supplication to a God we do not understand.

The Mass offers us more.

Confiteor Deo quia peccavi.

Praying for forgiveness takes us back over what we have done and have failed to do. With my mind too full to consider what I had failed to do, it drifted to what I have done. It went back to a day 45 years ago on a tennis court near Cleveland where I met Suzanne. She was not as good at tennis as other activities — raising three children, earning three degrees from UD, managing a clinical laboratory, making my eyes open to the wonders of creation, to many reasons to give glory to God.

Adoramus te.

In addition to memories, into my prayer at the 12:05 intruded questions. Who were these other few score people there? Supplicants like me? Or those who routinely praise their God? Or maybe some had come in thanksgiving? A recent *UDQ* item sparked one UD grad to seek out and thank a teacher of 60 years ago. His gratitude reminded me to send belated thanks to a teacher whose wisdom stayed with me for decades.

And now, with Suzanne's surgery successfully completed, I join with others who thank their fellow humans for caring and kindness and thank God for all-embracing love.

Gratias agimus tibi.

Per saecula saeculorum.

Amen.

ALWAYS, THE RIVER

As the elder of the office, I have the curmudgeonly obligation to trim the sails of Pollyannish optimism. For example, this venerable institution — that has employed me throughout my adult life thus providing food, shelter and education for my family — like other organizations on the move talks much of change.

Not all change is good. It is not good when a friend's cells embark on growing with cancerous intensity. It is not good when a family business of UD alumni transforms through fire into ashes. It is not good — at least in temporal sense for those of us left behind — when death gnaws at our University community.

Even on a less profound level, adapting to change can be hard for some of us. My son does not cope well with Milano's menu changes. An older grad wistfully remembers Dottie's. Another tries to remember what Tank's was before that location was one of the incarnations of the Walnut Hills — for that was where a young lady, now respectably retired, danced one night upon a table.

For better or for worse, change is a constant of our lives. So, for every look back, perhaps we had best take at least one forward.

For every look back at the Wright brothers or Dunbar or Patterson, we here on the banks of the Great Miami River should envision what might become. Will UD's venture into public education (in a building once home to manufacturing might) nurture minds that will — like Wright and Dunbar and Patterson — soar and sing and sell? Will land infused with the spirit of departed American factory workers be the future site for researchers discovering materials to fuel America's economic engines?

One direction UD is looking in the future is west. The land UD has purchased from NCR extends the former core campus westward to the river. On the west bank of the river, UD has developed a 30-acre athletic complex, home to teams picking up phrases like "best" and "record-breaking."

Dayton as a city is also looking west. Residential, commercial and medical development after decades' hiatus has appeared on the city's near West Side. The river once nearly destroyed the city and the city turned its back upon it. Now the river may be bringing the city together. Maybe it will also bring together its people.

That would be a welcome change.

WEDDING PHOTOS

The team that puts class notes together for *UDQ* includes Jeaneen Parsons, the office production manager, who organizes them; Maureen Schlangen, who writes them from her home; and Matt Dewald, who edits the *UDQ* alumni section when he's not editing the *Dayton Educator* or other publications.

Unlike their counterparts at many alumni publications who shy away from using wedding photos in class notes, this team sees no problem using them on a space-available basis.

Good reasons exist for not running such photos: Even the most beautiful brides aren't very striking when their faces are an eighth of an inch high. And giving space to such ordinary events as weddings takes away from the really important things universities do to transform the world.

Recently I snapped a photo (too late for this issue's deadline) of a couple of dozen UD grads at the wedding of my son Mike. I also hold strong views on what's really important and on how the world is transformed.

I believe some of that transformation is being done by my wife, Suzanne, as she manages a hospital laboratory, by my daughter, Elizabeth, as she teaches eighth-graders, by Mike as he practices law and by tens of thousands of other UD grads as they daily live their lives.

Mike's bride, Jenn, presented Suzanne and me with a gift. Inscribed on a plate were the names of both families and the wedding date with a quotation: "Other things change us, but we start and end with family."

Weddings occasion much thought of families. Jenn and Mike each thought of family members whom the other had not been able to meet and love because of the separation of death. They thought of those who overcame the separation of distance to be with them. They thought of mothers and daughters, fathers and sons, brothers and sisters — in both literal and metaphorical senses.

Such thoughts, such gatherings bind together people who may not seem to be changing the world. But those wedding pictures, those class notes, they are the news of a people who attended a school founded by a religious order influenced deeply by a woman who seemed just like other women — because she was. But like all other men and women, she was unique. In her case, she was the mother of God.

But for believing Christians, she and we are all just part of the family — and as family we can change the world.

'DID TOOTS DIE?'

With the pressure of deadline compressing hours of reading-interviewing-organizing-writing-talking-proofreading about learning-inspiring-perspiring-living-loving-dying, Friday night was an opportunity for decompression with loyal spouse and loving granddaughters.

Deciding to end the evening with a movie, we happened upon *Lassie Come Home* (1943), which in addition to spawning decades of sequels, television shows and tacky collie bric-a-brac turned out to be an engaging film.

With so many sequels, I guessed that Lassie would make it home unlike the rabid dog that Megan saw in a movie that day at school. That dog was taken out and shot, making a deep impression on first-graders.

Near the beginning of *Lassie Come Home*, the young boy's father says, "You can't feed a dog on the dole, and you can't feed a family either." Early on we know both why Lassie must be sold and what is important — family.

All that's left is for Lassie to make it back from Scotland to his Yorkshire home and for the family to live happily ever after. No, not quite. The film's set in the Depression and made during World War II. Staying alive and having a job were sufficient family goals.

Lassie on her perilous journey home encounters so many solid Englishmen that, if Hitler would have seen the film, he'd have surrendered. One stalwart who befriends Lassie is a kind peddler who travels in his cart with his tiny dog, Toots. Robbers attack the peddler. With the dogs' help, he drives them off. But Toots after the attack lies still.

"Did Toots die?" Megan asks simply.

The answer is, of course, simple. But as she and her younger sister Molly (sound asleep at this point) continue their lifelong journey of learning-inspiring-perspiring-living-loving-dying, the answers will get more complex. Ours that Friday did not include the dedication of the movie to the Yorkshire-born novelist who fought in the British Army in World War I and died a major in the U.S. Army before the film's release and sometime between the wars found time to write and also to bond, not with a small dog, but with a collie called Toots. The answer did not include this reminding me of writing about World War II veterans in UD's family and about today's students and thinking of tomorrow's realities.

But that would be for another day. On that Friday, it was enough to know that the loyal Toots fought and died and Lassie came home.

THE EMPTY TOMB

One knows the day is special when Chris Duncan shows up in a suit. The Third Sunday of Easter this year was special for a number of people at the 10 a.m. Mass for which Duncan, chair of the political science department, did one of the readings.

That morning was an ending.

It was an ending for Patti and Allen Stock, retiring after two decades at UD as music ministers. For them and for the volunteers who formed the choir at this Mass, it was a farewell.

So, too, was it a farewell for the celebrant, Father Jim Heft, S.M., a fixture at this Mass since 1979, about to depart on a three-year leave to Southern California. As celebrant of this Sunday morning Mass, he noted to the assembled congregation, he followed in the footsteps of Father Edwin Leimkuhler, S.M., perhaps most famous for his role in the conversion of Erma Fiste Bombeck to Catholicism.

UD's past was palpable in the chapel that morning both in memories and in the presence of those there, such as Brother John Lucier, S.M., famed chemistry professor, and Martha Baker, widow of the legendary philosophy chair, Richard Baker. And there were the rest of the congregation — theologians and engineers, townspeople and academics, the elderly and the newly baptized as well as the editor of this periodical and the alto to whom he is married and who has brought harmony both to the melodies of the choir and to the troubles of his soul.

Of our troubled souls, Heft had spoken two weeks earlier, on Easter morning, when he directed us to the verses after those in the day's reading, to Mary Magdalene saying with tears, "They have taken away my Lord, and I know not where they have laid him." And one could almost sense tears in the priest's voice as he spoke of Mary's fear and confusion before the empty tomb — until Jesus called her name and she recognized him.

And at Heft's last Mass, he talked of other signs, of recognizing the Lord in the breaking of bread, of community — both his Marianist brothers and the assembled worshippers whom he told, "Never underestimate the impact you have on the life of a priest."

And we went forth knowing that when we weep at the empty tomb, we weep for ourselves. But when we recognize the grace God pours upon us, we exalt with all His creation.

A SPECIAL PLACE

A former colleague stopped by the office recently. She remarked how she enjoyed coming back to UD's campus. It struck me then how much the appearance of this place has changed over the years. I remember the late B.J. Bedard, the chair of the English department who first hired me at UD, talking about serving on the committee that planned the construction of the library now named after Father Raymond A. Roesch, S.M.

B.J. said the committee allotted all the funding to the building, assuming that somebody would come up with money for landscaping. Somebody did. But it took years.

As a better-endowed University now constructs and remodels its impressive physical plant, landscaping is not an afterthought. Keller Hall came with a new entrance to the University. Marianist Hall and the RecPlex blend in so well one has trouble remembering where Founders Field was. Flowers and plants abound.

But this wasn't what my former colleague meant.

UD's campus, she explained, was distinct because of God's presence here.

She said that here people bring God into the classrooms and the curriculum, into their work and their lives.

Perhaps some days we are too close to the details of our work and problems to notice that presence, but the sacramental nature of this institution, its signs, its symbols are never far from us. Some — like Serenity Pines next to the Marianist cemetery or the new Mary garden next to the Chapel of the Immaculate Conception — are in the landscape itself.

Some are less visible, such as the work of a faculty group trying to define what a UD education should be. Part of what they have elaborated as a mission states that UD students "pursue rigorous academic inquiry, in a sacramental spirit, and engage in vigorous dialogue, learning in, through, and for community."

A couple of thousand years of Catholic tradition and centuries of Marianist experience give us an extraordinary perspective when it comes to figuring out "learning in, through, and for community."

And this community, this place, this people give us an extraordinary opportunity to be sign, to be symbol, to be a means whereby the Creator, the Alpha, the Omega, is a transforming presence in a world yearning for a love that is eternal.

DISAGREEMENTS

If you ever met Stan Saxton, he might have seemed the kind of guy who, if you said Player A was the greatest baseball player ever, would say, "What about Player B?" And you'd be forced to come up with facts about Player A and reasons why these were more significant than Player B's stats. And you'd share not so much an argument as a passion.

Saxton was passionate about the University of Dayton.

Although he died in 1999, his name came up at this year's first faculty meeting. What with a new strategic plan and land-use planning and looking at curriculum, UD is embarking on a period of what some might politely call "discussions." Others might say "arguments." Around here they are often called "conversations."

At the meeting, faculty members attentively listened as Provost Fred Pestello talked of "The Perpetuation of Excellence: Celebration, Grand Initiatives, and Supportive Engagement." Their attention intensified as he offered Saxton as a single example of "our Marianist model of treating each other respectfully through the course of our deliberations, and not letting disagreements negatively affect relationships."

Pestello, noting that Saxton was "dedicated, respected and outspoken," said, "During the time I served as chair of the department to which we belonged, Stan and I sometimes saw things differently, occasionally very differently."

He then recalled a summer's day after he had moved on to being an associate dean. Saxton and he, standing in the Pestello driveway, reminisced about their spirited disagreements. As their talk concluded, Saxton looked at Pestello, said "You were always right," hugged him, got into his car and drove off.

"At the time," Pestello said, "I believed his words. ... Today, I know better." But he also knows what it's like to have a compassionate, caring, confidence-inspiring colleague.

Departmental discussions, talks in driveways — these are places for what Father Paul Vieson, S.M., called "the little courtesies" as he preached in October at the Mass of Christian Burial of professor emeritus of history Wilfred Steiner. Steiner, too, was a man who knew, in Vieson's words, "what the little kindnesses can mean and the good they inspire. Easter comes to us, most often, in the common, the mundane actions of life. Only once did it come in infinite glory and that was enough. We must be Easter to others in the ordinary events of our lives."

EAGLES

On Jan. 20 a Blackhawk helicopter crashed near Baghdad. A dozen soldiers died. One was Col. Paul Kelly.

He was, as the University's announcement of his death said, "one of our own." Many of us knew his father, John, a grad who worked here in career placement for many years after also serving his country. Col. Kelly himself graduated in 1984. Also UD grads are his sisters, Brita '84 and Therese '85, and his brothers, John '85, Patrick '90 and Tony '95.

Col. Kelly was commissioned through UD's ROTC program and held numerous leadership positions in the National Guard, serving in Ohio, South Carolina and Virginia. His assignments took him to the Pentagon, to Bosnia and to Iraq.

In remembering Kelly, a sergeant said, "I would walk behind him in any war, in any place." At a memorial service a four-star general spoke of Kelly as if he were his brother.

Kelly was buried at Arlington National Cemetery with full military honors. Before 21 guns saluted and the bugler played, the fallen soldier was honored by a squadron of slow-moving, low-altitude Blackhawk helicopters.

Jerry Walsh '87, an Alpha Nu Omega brother of Kelly's who attended the ceremony, wrote how he was impressed by it but even more so by what he witnessed on the bus ride after. "I was sitting next to a group of enlisted Army soldiers, and they were uncontrollably sobbing. … The genuine respect and admiration of the soldiers you command is the real testament of a successful leader."

At the Mass celebrated for Kelly at St. William of York Catholic Church, the congregation sang of ultimate success:

And He will raise you up on eagles' wings,
bear you on the breath of dawn,
make you to shine like the sun,
and hold you in the palm of His hand.

Behind Col. Kelly's desk he had hung a large eagle picture. He called his troops his Eagles. And he called his children — Paul, 9, and John, 5 — his little eagles.

As the plane carrying Kelly's body home had landed earlier in Virginia, so too — near where the family had gathered — had landed a bird, a bald eagle. It stayed until the body was transferred into a hearse. And then it flew away.

SIGNS AND WONDERS

The end is near. At least that is what some folk conclude when they see the world's palpable evils. They see the sin and death about us as signs of imminent apocalypse.

The UD students pictured on Page 5, however, not only literally hold a sign of their bond with counterparts at Virginia Tech but also — in their coming together to do that and pray — are themselves a hopeful sign.

The Medal of Honor that Col. Gordon Roberts (Page 31) has quietly held for years is also a sign of a bond. So are places — houses with their porches or the Chapel of the Immaculate Conception.

Evil may be palpable, but so is the good that binds us together. That is something that Father Norbert Burns, S.M., (Page 19) has reminded us of for more than six decades of teaching Christian Marriage.

As *UDQ* is arriving in alumni homes, alumni will be traveling to campus for reunion, many of them to renew their wedding vows in the chapel, again giving testament to the power of divine and human love.

Our own family is celebrating sacraments this spring. Megan Taylor Goheen, whose parents plan in June to be among those renewing their vows in the chapel, received her first Holy Communion. The priest asked the children assembled with their families what was unusual about that day. In addition to the sacrament, there were other signs — fancy clothes, visiting relatives, nice gifts and, the priest reminded them, parties. Parties, too, are signs. We gathered, we celebrated, we were sign to Megan and the world.

We are gathering again, this time to welcome Caroline Johanna Columbus into the Church. Five months old, she does not understand the language of sacrament, of instrument and sign. But there are times when understanding is perhaps best left to God.

If you have read this *UDQ* from back to front, you already know of another young girl looking into her future and watching a note in a bottle float off toward the sea. Now as a graduating senior, she can write of a University that attracts people who are "not only aware of the vastness of the world around them, but also the details, the little things in life which really turn out to be the biggest things."

Of the grad who found her note, she can say, "He saw in that message the dream of a child and realized he could be part of something greater, something beautiful and mysterious."

People, unknown to each other, willing to reach out. Good signs.

THE ANSWER

Our children would have been mortified if we had ever had a "My child is an honor student at …" bumper sticker. But for a moment at Reunion Weekend I thought it would be neat to have one that read, "My daughter got an 'A' in Father Burns' class."

We didn't expect to be in the Immaculate Conception Chapel that day this June when alumni were renewing their wedding vows and new Golden Flyers were being inducted. We were baby-sitting grandchildren Megan and Molly.

But the phone rang. Daughter Liz said her husband, Tony, was saving seats, front-row no less.

So there we were — grandparents and granddaughters and their parents — in chapel seats near where decades ago we had sat with Megan and Molly's mother and uncles. A close examination of a photograph in the new Heritage Center reveals us in a scene from one of those Masses, frozen in time near that same place in the chapel.

Self-consciously we realized this June day we were rather underdressed in comparison to the Golden Flyers, to whom we were closer in age than the more casually dressed younger alumni. But we did have two young girls with us, keeping us young, as grandparents like to say.

We didn't expect to be there. But, as throughout all our lives, much of what we remember as important is what we did not expect.

In this issue's Perceptions, a former colleague, Kate Cassidy Harrison, writes of digging up at Reunion Weekend a time capsule she and her friends buried before graduation. What one expected 20 years ago is often not what today has brought. As you read this issue, can you imagine what Herbie Dintaman expected when he came to UD as a young football coach or what Sean Wilkinson expected as a young photographer or what a century of residents of the "Castle" expected or what William Joseph Chaminade thought would come of the communities he nurtured?

We can hope and prepare for what is to come, but we cannot see it.

As we face the unexpected, we have symbols and signs to mark the way — fire and water, bread and wine. And rings.

The priest who helped thousands learn of Christian marriage asks what does the ring symbolize. The daughter — born of love, marrying in love, mothering in love — learned the answer years ago and remembers it well.

The ring is never ending.

As is God who is love.

WINNING

Tony Dungy really believes God wants the Indianapolis Colts to win.

Opening a homily on the 29th Sunday in Ordinary Time with that statement gained Father Joseph Tedesco, S.M., the attention of the 10 a.m. congregation in the Chapel of the Immaculate Conception. It reminded me of saying victory rosaries decades ago and of a high school football loss to Holy Name that led some to question the efficacy of prayer if not the existence of God.

As a priest and a sport psychology researcher, Tedesco has a more profound interest in and deeper understanding of the subject.

The gospel of that Sunday certainly stressed the power of prayer. A widow seeking justice keeps bothering a dishonest judge. ("Gives him a black eye," Tedesco said is the literal translation.) Because of that, the judge gives her a just decision. Luke tells us, "The Lord said, Pay attention to what the dishonest judge says. Will not God then secure the rights of his chosen ones who call out to him day and night?"

Among sport psychologists, however, some have seen prayer and spirituality in sports as, at best, ritual or, at worst, superstition. Others have seen benefits such as relaxation or team-building or a way of explaining defeat ("God's will").

Tedesco is among a new breed of researchers who see a more positive way of thinking about God and oneself as an athlete. He told the congregation the story of a man on a journey. It was difficult. People tried to talk him out of it; they didn't understand its importance. He himself seemed to constantly question his choice, his destination. But he continued.

The story, as Tedesco said, is "Luke's travel narrative. Christ has set his face to Jerusalem." Christ continues to Jerusalem, Tedesco said, "because he believes God believes in him."

According to Tedesco, an athlete understands being gifted and so "becomes egocentric or believes all gifts come from God." The power of that belief, in terms of athletics, can be an increased belief in self and thus increased performance, a phenomenon that Tedesco and his students are attempting to measure and to study.

From belief in God can come belief in self. "And, even when I don't believe in God," Tedesco said, "God believes in me and why would God believe in something that could not be victorious?"

WHY A BAPTIST, HERE?

Jordan Rowan Fannin thought it odd we had chosen her to be in a magazine ad for the religious studies department's graduate program. Why would a Catholic school pick a Baptist student to be part of its image?

To me the answer was simple: Jordan's academic interests focus on questions of community and neighborhoods, and she serves as a graduate assistant in the Fitz Center for Leadership in Community.

And UD's welcoming diversity isn't new. For example, while working on the ad, I was also researching John Q. Sherman (for one of the UD families stories that begin on Page 12). As Sherman campaigned for UD during the Depression, he pointed out not only UD's Catholic identity but also that 40 percent of the student body then was non-Catholic. "Everyone," he said, "is welcomed to the University irrespective of creed."

Even women were welcomed on an equal basis with men, a rarity in the 1930s.

Jordan's question, however, occasioned one of my own: Why would a Baptist come to study theology at a Catholic school?

In addition to her interest in community, Jordan had a simple answer for being in UD's master's program — her husband, Coleman, is in its doctoral program. So what brought him to UD?

At Baylor University, he had written his master's thesis on Dorothy Day and the Catholic Worker Movement. He wanted to study more of Catholic theology. He also wanted to study ethics. So he visited UD. Apparently, when prospective grad students visit, they react the same as prospective undergrads. He said he liked what he saw, "the atmosphere, the collegiality."

Andy Black, another Baylor-educated Baptist in the religious studies doctoral program, said that when he visited he "was attracted by the interdisciplinary focus, the emphasis on the U.S. Catholic experience."

He saw people here trying to understand the lives of Christians in a certain tradition in a certain culture. They were asking, he said, "questions similar to those I had been asking myself as a Baptist. We may have been coming from different directions but were asking ourselves what it meant to be a Christian in the United States."

As doctoral students, Andy and Coleman look forward to teaching careers. As seminary grads, they see teaching as a form of service. And that is another attraction at UD, where, Coleman said, "the focus is not just academic. It's academic in service to the church."

LOVE LETTERS

In the 17 years of *UDQ*'s existence, you've read often in this space about death. With the first issue, it was an obvious choice. Father Raymond A. Roesch, S.M., longtime UD president, had died. Over the years, you've read here of many other deaths. Words here have tried to react to the deaths of students and alumni, famous and anonymous, of colleagues and neighbors, of old Marianists and of my youngest child.

Sometimes the subjects have been happier. A colleague once advised me, "Write about Megan" — my oldest and, at that time, my only granddaughter. And it wasn't very hard to write of a child whose first sentence was "Go, UD!" And it wouldn't be hard now to write of her and her sister, Molly, and their cousin, Caroline.

But what is the point of these 17 years of words of death and birth, of past and future? Are we simply acknowledging the observation of a Greek philosopher, himself long dead, that change is the only constant?

We don't need people to see that. Even these pages provide testimony to that. They don't fall out like they used to; the ink doesn't come off on your hands, does it? And, the next time you see them, they will be transformed substantially.

So why probe the pain of death or reveal the depth of personal feeling? An answer was expressed in that first *UDQ* column in its first two words: "Amazing grace." God's grace is with us constantly, but most of us don't daily open our eyes to it. Death, whatever else it may be, is an eye-opener. So are children.

With our eyes open, we see beyond surfaces. In others, we see God. Theologians talk of the concept of sacramentality, the revelation of God to us through creation. Maybe it is simpler to talk of love, which can appear in the oddest places.

Our managing editor found it in this issue's only feature: "100 Things We Love About UD." He had an epiphany: Each one of these items is a love letter to UD alumni. I, too, had an epiphany: That this issue was born of love, the love of UD by the art director (reputedly even more curmudgeonly than I) who conceived of the idea, the managing editor who nurtured it, the others of us here who wrote and photographed, the alumni who contributed. Somehow such a coming together as a loving community to express such love seems to be a very UD thing to do.

But those of you who went to school here already know that.

May God bless and keep you.

CHANGE

Twenty-five hundred years ago, a dead Greek reportedly observed (before he died) that everything is in a state of flux.

To confuse generations (or perhaps provoke them to thought), Heraclitus said things like, "We both step and do not step in the same rivers. We are and are not." So, if yesterday you found it a treat to beat your feet in the Mississippi mud and if you try that again today, is the river the same? Are you?

Blessed William Joseph Chaminade also had some things to say about change. In post-revolutionary France, he believed that "new times called for new methods." He, like Heraclitus, used a metaphor of flowing water. He compared how he was going to do his work to a brook encountering an obstacle. The obstacle blocks the flow for a time, but the brook grows wider and deeper and flows around the obstacle.

The University of Dayton continues the tradition of the ancient philosopher by reflecting on the nature of change. It continues the tradition of Chaminade by effecting change, and by transforming the world.

All three of the features in this issue touch on change.

An article on visual satire and politics emerged from a presidential campaign in which both sides tried to grab the mantle of change.

Often change comes too fast to cope with. Not long ago cybercrime was not much more than a concept; today it may siphon more than $1 trillion a year from the U.S. economy. But that may not be as serious as potential cyberthreats to national security. NCR Distinguished Professor of Law and Technology Susan Brenner sees the way responses to cyberthreats are ineffective.

Real threats faced the African village where a group of UD civil engineering students spent a good part of their summer. The village lacked safe drinking water. The UD students thought they could change that. So they went to Africa to try.

From just picking up this magazine, you will have noticed that change is not just the subject of our features but of form and content throughout. What you see and read here results from a consulting relationship with 160over90, the Philadelphia branding agency responsible for *Transformative Moments* (UD's president's report) and for the recent award-winning publications of UD's division of enrollment management.

New sections in the magazine include Expert Instruction on Page 6 and an essay by President Daniel J. Curran on our last page, Page 64.

Another new section, The Big Question, poses a question for readers. This one — on how to spend $2 billion to change the world — was posed to readers of the e-mail newsletter *New from UDQ*. Of the more than 150 answers received, the largest number dealt with providing basic needs, such as food and, primarily, water.

So, the change brought by current UD students to an African village is also a change envisioned by numbers of UD alumni. Perhaps the river that is UD, in which alumni stepped years ago, is some way the same transforming experience for those who are students now.

Living Relics

Everybody can find something odd in other people's religions. Sometimes we see parts of our own to be odd. That was the case when I raised the possibility that this issue's Hidden Treasure piece might feature a relic residing on campus. After the obligatory disclaimer that I was not referring to myself, it became clear that many of our readers would find relics odd. (Some of you may find the dominoes that became the issue's Hidden Treasure on Page 61 a bit odd, too; but that's another story.)

The word "relic" comes from a Latin verb meaning to leave behind; for Catholics, a relic is something a saint or martyr left behind — perhaps clothing or even part of a body that in life served as a temple of the Holy Spirit.

A veneration for tangible things may seem unusual to those who see religion as rising above the material to seek the spiritual. Gathering pieces of bone or bits of cloth associated with dead people may seem to them more like collecting baseballs signed by Babe Ruth or parts of a car driven by James Dean. (That is a gruesome story in itself, as John Heitmann — whose love of the automobile is featured beginning on Page 18 — can tell you.)

And maybe in some ways such activity is odd. But we are human beings, not disembodied spirits. We see physical matter; we hear audible sounds; we remember them; we think about them. We make sounds and develop them into symbols, into words; we see in objects something beyond their material form; we thrive with signs that stretch us.

The connections we make are sometimes unpredictable — such as mine were when I visited the Holocaust Memorial Museum. The story that place tells is monumental and vast. Yet what moved me to tears was a small, simple display of scores of black, furled umbrellas — simple objects, taken from those led to slaughter, symbols of their daily, ordinary lives, symbols of sacred individual human beings.

One of the names in this issue's In Memoriam is that of another sacred individual, Bud Cochran, whose life can be remembered in symbols — the hole blasted in his World War II destroyer, the Native American medal he wore as a professor, the food that he as a St. Vincent volunteer delivered in retirement.

Another name in that list is Ellie Kurtz. Every December, an event she founded — Christmas on Campus — offers a symbol of the nature of our University in the faces of University of Dayton students and in the faces of those Dayton students who come to campus each December from schools and communities such as those described in this issue's feature starting on Page 28.

These ordinary things that we see in our daily lives have meaning. In the faces of those with whom we come in mundane contact, we see not just the worldly. We see in them the sacred.

And if we look hard enough, we may indeed see the face of God and live.

RESOUNDING GONGS, GO AWAY

We are a country at odds with itself. We often see those with whom we disagree as conspiring to destroy the America we love. At our worst, our disagreements lend fodder to those who scoff at the notion of democracy.

So, we here take a little pride that this issue presents at least one story (more, we hope) that may make you not only proud to be associated with the University of Dayton but also proud to be an American and proud just to be a member of the human race. They are stories of conflict from Vietnam to the Middle East and within our own country. But they are also stories of hope and comrades, of community and family.

The topics are lofty, perhaps; the lives of some of the people, larger than life as we know it in our everyday lives. But in those everyday lives lies the seed of what is substantial. On this campus, that seed is nourished by a "front-porch" mentality that students experience, whether being welcomed by a fellow student on a real front porch or being welcomed anywhere in this community. One of the guidebooks to colleges refers to UD as "academically challenging yet unpretentious." It's fitting that the actions of those at a school called Catholic testify to the words of St. Paul that "love is not pompous, it is not inflated, it is not rude."

We reflect on such love at milestone events like graduations and weddings and funerals. Lately, I haven't been to many graduations or weddings but have been reminded of the words of an aging Brother Elmer Lackner, S.M., (an administrator with so many roles he was just called "Mr. UD"), who, when asked what he did, noted he was at a point where he mainly went to funerals. And I've been reminded that funeral gatherings cut through pretensions and focus us on what is fundamental. Sometimes what we see is so obvious we haven't really seen it for awhile.

At a viewing recently for the mother of a colleague, the family remarked how wonderful it was that so many of my colleague's co-workers had come to the viewing. … An alumna friend of ours recently sat with her comatose mother slowly slipping into death. The friend sang hymns to ears that some might say could not hear. … At yet another recent funereal gathering, UD folk talked of the happy times, of alumni gathering in distant cities, of people who accepted and cared for one another, of porches real and metaphorical.

Maybe these actions aren't odd or earthshaking. But they are what good people, like the people of UD, do. Often, it amounts to just being there.

So, perhaps should we celebrate even more the opportunities we have for being there, for being together. Being there, being together, is not insignificant. We cannot explain that significance. But then neither can we explain the Trinity, that overwhelming mystery of relationship that informs our Christian universe.

It is, however, a mystery that informs every point of time in our lives, that maybe explains why we ask the mother of God to pray for us "now and at the hour of our death. Amen."

HOPES AND MEMORIES

My colleagues joke that I was here when Father Leo Meyer, S.M., bought John Stuart's farm and started a school. Not quite, I sneer. But I was on campus when the building in which I now work was part of the thriving factory complex of the National Cash Register Company.

Professors then used to time their leaving campus so as to avoid 4 p.m. Those of us near the top of Miriam Hall could see — at the exact striking of the hour — the doors of those factories fly open and thousands of workers flow out on their way home. Many of those same workers took time out of their lunch breaks to attend at Holy Angels a Mass that, in keeping with their time constraints, lasted but 20 minutes.

My memories don't go back to 1923 when workers living in nearby houses came to the rescue of the few students remaining on campus at the beginning of Christmas break and drove off hundreds of bomb-placing, cross-burning, Catholic-hating Klansmen.

I do remember, however, that neighborhood changing. The workers gradually disappeared, replaced by students. National Cash Register became NCR as its business evolved. More than the company's name shrank as manufacturing in Dayton dwindled. And last year NCR moved its headquarters south.

Over time, the neighborhoods that once housed factory workers have become part of UD. Brown Street businesses flourish once again. Flyer athletic facilities have blossomed on the west side of the Great Miami River. And in 2005 the University expanded its acreage dramatically by buying the old NCR factory site, which lay between the historic campus and the Arena Sports Complex. Recently, the University made an even more dramatic move with an even larger purchase, including NCR's former world headquarters, just to the south of the 2005 parcel.

We don't have to explain that these acquisitions are a big deal. Opportunities like these don't come along in just any century.

Father Meyer saw one in the mid-19th century, when having come to Ohio to help with a cholera epidemic, he bought land from a farmer who, grieving the death of his infant daughter, wished to return to his native land. Another farm, just to the west of his, the Pattersons', would see the genesis, growth and departure of an industrial giant, NCR.

Although that organization has moved on, the University of Dayton isn't leaving; it's building a future here.

That fact, as our cover story illustrates, is not only good news for Daytonians but also part of a trend of major universities taking leading roles in their regions' economic development.

The land's change in ownership provides an occasion for what a former cover of ours proclaimed as "Hopes and Memories" — a phrase we have since realized we could use on any cover of this magazine. For that is what we try to share with you, the reader. This issue has some fond memories of athletics and athletes and alumni. It has some bittersweet ones of NCR. And it has some terrifying ones of human enslavement.

But the issue is full of hope — for victims of human trafficking, for the success of the Flyers and for the future of this University as it strives to transform itself, its region and its world.

Amazing Grace

When each of us came first to Dayton, we came holding hopes for our futures. But we did not know what those futures would hold.

When Kristi Kerscher came from Toledo to Dayton as a student 20-some years ago, she was not planning to live in Australia; but you can read in this issue about her now being premier of that country's largest state. When I came to Dayton in 1967, I was not planning to edit and write about the University of Dayton for most of my life. My wife, Suzanne, and I intended to stay here for a year while she finished her education degree and I picked up teaching experience in UD's English department. Then we were going to move on somewhere with me continuing work on a doctoral degree.

My wife got her UD degree. I got my experience; teaching in the late 1960s was certainly an experience. But by 1973, I was no longer teaching, no longer pursuing a Ph.D. And we were still in Dayton.

Decades have passed. I've written and edited much. Suzanne has acquired two more degrees and a career in health care. We have marveled at the births of our children, rejoiced at weddings and marveled again at the births of grandchildren.

Our joys and sorrows have been shared by colleagues at this wondrous place, this University of Dayton. These people have enhanced the exhilaration of success; and, when plans have collapsed, they have made life livable.

One vivid memory of the community of my colleagues is of some of them sitting around my dining room table as we planned an issue of this periodical. While we talked, my younger son came home from high school, greeted us all and went off to do the things that 15-year-olds do. Less than a month later, he died. I still have my notes and story plans from that meeting. And I have the memories of the community that supported and support our family.

This space has often spoken of death and community and love and the grace of God that holds it all together. Our first words here in 1991, reacting to the death of long-time president Father Raymond A. Roesch, S.M., were "amazing grace."

And it is indeed amazing.

Today, the future, as ever, is uncertain. The world worries about money. In my professional world, lovers of Catholic universities worry about secularization of those institutions. Faculties worry about communities of scholars losing their souls to corporatization.

We all have our fears.

We might think of Mary's fears when an angel told her she was going to become the mother of God. Or her fears at the foot of the cross when her dying son told her that the disciple who loved him was now her son and she, his mother. We might think of the fear of the disciples before Pentecost. And what of their fears at Pentecost itself? And in the millennia that have followed?

But, the wonder of it all is that grace will surely see us through.

Thomas M. Columbus
Editor